T0128333

BUSINESS CHARACTER
MATTERS

THE TEN HABITS OF HIGHLY SUCCESSFUL MANAGERS

DERRICK JORDAN

authorHOUSE®

AuthorHouse™
1663 Liberty Drive
Bloomington, IN 47403
www.authorhouse.com
Phone: 1 (800) 839-8640

Published by AuthorHouse 10/04/2019

ISBN: 978-1-7283-3049-5 (sc)
ISBN: 978-1-7283-3047-1 (hc)
ISBN: 978-1-7283-3048-8 (e)

Library of Congress Control Number: 2019915710

Print information available on the last page.

Scripture quotations marked NKJV are taken from the New King James Version. Copyright © 1982 by Thomas Nelson, Inc. Used by permission. All rights reserved.

This book is printed on acid-free paper.

PRAISE FOR

Business Character Matters

"Highly recommended for new managers, those thinking of a career in management, and the manager who feels like they want to take their career to the executive level. Invaluable, well-written, and informative!"

—**Gregory Collins**
Author, *The Great Things You'll Do!*

"A must for every manager—new and experienced. A wise, character-developing book. Hands down, one of the best and most powerful management books I have read and recommended to countless managers and executives. This book caused me to break out my highlighter and notepad."

—**Dennis L. Richardson**
Author, *Above and Beyond: Leading and Managing Organizational Change*

"Being a Navy engineering manager, I've tried several management techniques, but nothing seemed to move my passion. This book taught me the habits to achieve a winning character and enormous results."

—**Jack Hopson, Jr.**
Author, *Naval Engineering: The Principles of Fire Protection*

CONTENTS

DEDICATION

To my supportive and loving wife of seven years, Alsae L. Jordan, you have made me happy because I have found a true friend in you. You build me up and inspire me to live my life to the fullest. Thank you for listening to me when I open up enough to become vulnerable in sharing my dreams with you. I love you dearly.

To my most beloved children: son, Keagan; daughter, Keelia; and youngest son, DaMarcus. Continue to trust in and know that you have more courage, gifts, and intellect than you think. I know it might be hard to see it right now, but never give up on what you really desire to do. I love you with all that is within me—and then some!

ACKNOWLEDGMENTS

I would like to first extend my sincere thanks to all the successful managers who supported and encouraged me to write and publish this management book, specifically Gregory Collins, for his lifelong friendship, knowledge, and expertise.

Secondly, I humbly share this publication with the more than sixty-five managers and executives who contributed to "The Successful Manager" chapter. Your wisdom, experience, and professionalism will continue through the generations as many read your words. I am indebted to all of you. Thank you!

Lastly, thank you to the entire group of professionals at WellStar in Atlanta, Georgia. You are the most professional team I have ever had the pleasure of working with. You deserve all of the success life and career holds for you. Blessings!

*Cover photograph courtesy of Keith Hammock Photography.

DISCLAIMERS

The information or material contained in this book, including advice and opinions, are the author's own and do not reflect endorsement by or the views of WellStar, the Department of Defense, the United States Government, or the United States Department of the Navy. The author is solely responsible and liable concerning the content of this book. Although the words *he, him,* and *his* are used sparingly in this book to enhance communication, they are not intended to be gender driven or to be an affront to or discriminate against anyone reading this text.

Several unabridged and abridged public domain texts listed on the reference page have been heavily adapted, modified, revised, and edited to convey exact principles, concepts, or applications effectively. The author does not claim ownership, only compilation and editing.

PREFACE

Marshall Field was an American entrepreneur and the founder of Marshall Field and Company, the Chicago-based department store renowned for its then-exceptional level of quality and customer service. In October 1871, when his store had burned in the great Chicago fire, Eastern investors quickly contacted him, offering to supply whatever money he required to rebuild. Why would they offer? Was this a good business policy?

After all, his goods were gone, his building was ruined, and his business was disrupted. However, the investors knew Marshall Field. They knew his principles, his motives, and his habits—they knew his character. His business character was the basis of his credit before the fire, so why should an outside incident affect its security? The investors reasoned and justified their judgment—business character mattered.

The same reasoning always holds everywhere in business—in all circumstances. If you are being considered for business promotion, for example, your character will be the determining factor. Is she ambitious? Does he lead with confidence? Does she show initiative, act with invincible determination, and has she mastered self-control? Is he loyal? Is she consistent? Such questions as these must be asked and answered satisfactorily before any real decision can be made.

The individual of upright character is the trusted manager, the responsible executive, the leader in every field of business. Character is the highest component of personality. Physical and mental development alone is not enough. It is when these are completed with character development that an individual truly matters in an organization. He is a focused, unwavering, dependable, trustworthy, and powerful professional with business character.

INTRODUCTION

I t is wise to know what comes first and what to do first. To begin anything in the middle or at the end is to make a mess. The runner who began by breaking the finish line tape would not receive the prize. He must begin by facing the starter line and toeing the mark, and even then, a good start is important if he expects to win.

The first things in a professional manager—and therefore in a truly happy and successful business career—are *right habits*. Unless you start with right habits, wrong practices will follow, and a substandard and inadequate career will be the ending.

The Ten Habits of Highly Successful Managers are simple; yet without them, no real success or great accomplishment is achieved. To learn them thoroughly and to study how to apply them to all the details of career is to avoid confusion and to secure a substantial foundation for the orderly building up of an unshakable business character that matters.

To name the habits is easy; it is but mere words. However, managers must ensure these habits become fixed sources of action. I will deal with only ten business habits because they are the most common I have observed in successful managers over the past twenty-eight years. These ten habits are among the simplest, but they are those that come nearest to every business career. They touch the engineering, financial, medical, technology, science, and several other career fields at every point. The manager who perfects these habits will rise in the organization over many managers without them.

If you would believe that business character matters and truly practice The Ten Habits of Highly Successful Managers, your character and success are certain and secure. The ten habits are ten practices, ten avenues to achievement, and ten sources of knowledge. It is an old saying and a good rule that practice makes perfect. Do not merely read these habits aloud; you must establish them in your mind. To know them, and receive what they alone can bring, you must *do* them, and others must see them in your actions.

CHAPTER ONE

Business Character Matters

What is business character, and why is it important? Well, this story will assist in explaining.

Once, John Pierpont "JP" Morgan, the great banker and financier, gave a strong statement of the value of character as the foundation for credit in business during a Congressional investigation in Washington. While on the witness stand, Attorney Samuel Untermeyer asked Mr. Morgan if credit is based on money:

> "No, sir," replied Mr. Morgan, "it has no relation. I know lots of men—businessmen, too—who can borrow any amount, whose credit is unquestioned."

> "Is that not because it is believed that they have money backing them?" asked Mr. Untermeyer.

> "No, sir. It is because people believe in the man."

> "And is it, regardless of whether he has any financial backing at all?"

> "It is very often."

> "And he might not be worth anything?"

"He might not have anything. I have known a man to come into my office, and I have given him a check for a million dollars, and I knew that he had not a cent in the world."

"There are not many of them?"

"Yes, a good many."

"Are not commercial credits based upon possession of money or property?" inquired Mr. Untermeyer.

"No, sir, the first thing is a character," replied Mr. Morgan.

Mr. Morgan placed character first, and his evaluation is upheld even today by experience in every sector of business. It is always character that we take into consideration when arriving at a judgment of managers, organizations, and products in business.

Character is the determining quality, the litmus test, among managers because character means *consistency*. Just think for a moment: do you know where to find a manager of character? Can you predict his probable action in any situation because you know his habits of feeling and conduct? As Mr. Morgan's endorsement illustrates, the businessperson is wise to place more reliance on character than on money. Dollars without character are a waste; however, character itself is a priceless investment and can transform purpose, energy, and effort into material wealth.

Consider, for example, Tiffany & Company, the American luxury jewelry and specialty retailer. It was founded in 1837 by Charles Lewis Tiffany and John B. Young as a small elaborate goods store in lower New York. Its beginnings were humble; it was a modest shop, with several pretentious competitors. But the people who came to trade at Tiffany's soon found that all its dealings were characterized by an attitude of reliable trustworthiness that was always consistent, always to be depended upon.

The store never made extravagant claims for its goods; rather, it backed up its goods and service with a straightforward guarantee of quality. Thus customers came to know that they could count on Tiffany's word. This character was maintained through all the years as the business evolved from the modest shop into the imposing Fifth Avenue jewelry house it is today. Consistent habits of character and action resulted in success. While Tiffany's is renowned for its luxury goods and is principally known for its diamond and sterling silver jewelry, nothing matters more than its business character, which years of consistent action have developed.

Likewise, it is the same as with the manager. No wealth, no physical or mental ability is as valuable to you as good character. Character is the very essence of leadership in every realm of life and the mark of distinction in business. The manager of character is one who progressively moves ahead because his life is consistently stimulated by right motives and dominated by precise habits.

Character is the total of a manager's habits of feeling and action. It is the expression of the habits that guide and govern his life. Habits are the raw material of character. The manager who is careless of truth and honesty cannot have a moral character simply because he lacks the proper raw material.

If you know a manager's character, you can know, in advance, how she will feel and act under any circumstances. My childhood friend, a Navy engineering officer of thirty-two years, stated that he knows the character of his mechanics; therefore, he can forecast how each will act under stress and constant operation. Employers like WellStar Corporate know the character of their managers and entrust them with large responsibilities, trusting that under any circumstances they will uphold the highest character and bring credit upon the company.

The manager of character never surprises those who know him. His conduct in a given situation is inevitable. He is said to be consistent in emotions and actions. That is why the manager of character can call upon his practically unlimited resources of credit, as Mr. Morgan declared. That is why Tiffany's steadily grew in volume and quality. Character is a reputation that has been tested and approved.

Character is a plant of slow growth and is not something one can inherit ready-to-wear from parents. Because of your parent's integrity, others may trust you, expecting the right conduct; but it is their knowledge of the parent's character that gives them confidence. The final judgment of you is based on *your* actions—the way you express the habits that govern your life. A manager must build her character, and she builds it through the years as she forms her habits of emotion and will.

To achieve success in business, most people study business. However, the true prerequisite to success in business is first to study *yourself* and how to apply business to you. The human factor is the most important factor in the business world. Your character is one of the most crucial human factors. Thus, character matters.

Your character is dependent upon habits, and your habits are the foundation on which your success is built; therefore, character is essential. To achieve success, a manager develops the right habits for a success-winning character.

Success in business and success in character are two closely related achievements. Unfortunately, many equate success in business to money. True success, however, is possessing high character, of being beyond reproach. That is your goal if you want to be a successful business manager.

In the next section, you will discover success in business means far more than money. The Ten Habits of Highly Successful Managers highlight the role of character in determining success—meaning, the character of any manager can be developed into continuously greater success.

Over the years, character has been considered an ethical study rather than a business study, but with the rapid development of business, the true importance of character in the technological world is becoming understood.

In the pages that follow, I share the common habits two hundred managers and executives credit for their success. You will learn how to make these habits assets to your business life. You, too, can develop these attitudes to become more profitable and successful.

It does not matter what your current condition may be; you deserve to reach high levels of success in the business world. I spent twenty years serving in the United States Navy. In most cases, successful managers obtained opportunity based upon their character far more than their knowledge. Of the hundreds of managers I had the pleasure of consulting—many of whom achieved high positions in government, private, corporate, and entrepreneurial sectors—all have characters above reproach.

Success in character involves the study of habits, so research into why business character matters is vitally important. My investigation of the top-ten habits will not only increase your chances of obtaining gratification in business and social networks but will also grant you promotions and influence.

Managers have two powers that can be employed as they travel along the path of success: desire and will. As a manager, your desire and will to learn better habits will aid you in acquiring knowledge, developing power, achieving success, and finding gratification throughout your career and life.

CHAPTER TWO

The Ten Habits of Highly Successful Managers

Character is a product. It is not a natural donation bequeathed equally upon every manager—like twenty-four hours each day, or sunshine and rain. It is not some gift of Wisdom, distributed among a select business group. Character, the moral make-up of a manager, which dominates his feelings and actions, is produced by the underpinnings of his habits.

Your habits are who you are, and you are what you have willed to be. The failure to use will power to bring habits under control is chargeable to you, just as the positive use of will is also to your credit.

I once read that Abraham Lincoln developed the strong powers of his will at the age of twenty-one. Before that, he was a wandering, cheerful overgrown boy. If his will developed with use, then there had to be a beginning, a moment of decision. Before any achievement occurred, Lincoln decided to act.

First, it takes a decision; second, action must be applied. Decision and action are both included in will power, for no evidence of will exists apart from the action. Like Lincoln, you must decide to change and form new habits, character-building habits. Forming new, more productive habits may feel uncomfortable or unsettling at first, but persevere.

Every time an emotion is felt, it leaves its trace or mark on you. No matter how insignificant this trace seems, you must continue each repetition until the emotion finally becomes habitual and is one of the well-defined elements in your character. Repeated actions are performed more easily and with less thought or attention on your part. Habit and its repetition are vital actions in the development of The Ten Habits of Highly Successful Managers. The motto of highly successful managers is:

Sow an act, and you reap a habit.

Sow a habit, and you reap a character.

Sow a character, and you reap a destiny.

Just as it is possible to direct your habits of thinking, you can also direct your habits of feeling and action. As a manager, willpower is required to bring you to a decision and its accompanying action. After that, it is a matter of repetition, with each repetition requiring less will and effort.

The top-ten habits highly successful managers possess to propel them forward in business and win for them places of greater responsibility and leadership as executives are as follows:

1. Be Ambitious
2. Lead with Confidence
3. Display Loyalty
4. Know What You're Passionate About
5. Think Optimistically
6. Be Consistent
7. Get-Up-and-Go!
8. Act with Invincible Determination
9. Show Initiative
10. Master Self-Control

The fundamentals of business character are the total of these ten strong and active habits. It is not enough, for example, to be ambitious.

The ambitious manager who lacks confidence, initiative, and invincible determination is a stranded visionary, forever spinning castles in the air. The loyal manager who lacks consistency and get-up-and-go is a mere thinker who never puts his loyalty into practice. Therefore, master self-control and make these habits personal. Bear them in mind as you read and seek to apply them. You know your present character status; it is within your power to profit from this knowledge by eliminating every current weakness. You can gain complete mastery of yourself, by yourself and for yourself, so that you, too, can enjoy being a successful manager.

HABIT 1

Be Ambitious

After serving twenty years in the United States Navy, I cannot imagine a ship going out to sea without a chart and with no certain destination. I cringe at the thought of her sailing upon the great blue ocean with a full crew and a fair wind but with a captain who doesn't know where he is going. He knows hundreds of decent ports that would welcome his crew and give him honors; however, in hundreds of others, his crew may not be accepted. Without choosing a safe and certain destination, he follows the ever-changing breeze. He turns his ship into the wind and travels east. When the wind shifts north, he veers to the north; and when it blows west, he steers to the west.

Such a captain would be called insane. It is almost impossible for a reasoning mind to imagine such a situation. Yet, thousands of managers—captains of their destiny—are drifting on the business sea, aimlessly zigzagging before shifting winds, content if they stay afloat, merely surviving. They have never studied a chart of the business ocean; they have no destination in mind; they are drifters because they lack ambition.

What is ambition? It's not a simple wish for something, not the mere desire to rise higher in the world or to reach a goal. The young manager burning time and cigarettes on the company's gazebo bench while wishing for an executive job is not ambitious. Ambition is more than a desire, more than a sentimental longing. Ambition is a dynamic force, a committed drive to achieve.

Ambition comes from Latin, and its root meaning is "a going around after." In ancient days, a Roman seeking political office went around asking the citizens to vote for him, and because of his persistent action, he was called *ambitious.* A difference was apparent between an ambitious candidate and a passive one who desired office but made no positive efforts to attain it. Over the years, the word has broadened in meaning. Today, we call someone ambitious who sets a goal, deliberately plans and focuses, stretches every energy, and utilizes every legitimate means to reach it.

Your first step in developing the habit of ambition is to have a purpose, an object for your ambition, a clearly defined goal. You must desire to achieve, and you must know what it is that you wish to achieve. Common sense needs to be called into play here or else you may choose an unachievable goal, which will cause your failure.

No place in business is so high or so far that the truly ambitious and efficient manager may not reach it. With a clear goal, he can progress one step at a time. The manager who is ambitious for the senior vice president's vacancy is likely to lose sight of the intermediate steps, the long sequence of training and experience that he must pass through. Because he sets his first ambition too high, he may overestimate himself and overlook his real opportunity. That opportunity is the general manager, a position he could easily reach if he would devote himself to prepare for it.

Therefore, he should first be ambitious for a general manager position. Once he has achieved that position, he can then look ahead to the general manager of his region. He must set that goal as his new ambition; and if he is sincere in his purpose and diligent, it should come to fruition. Then, from the vantage point of the general manager's desk, he can look ahead to new worlds to conquer. Achieving has become a habit now, and he knows the power that lies within him.

Likewise, the company knows his power and will recognize him as a logical candidate for further promotion. When it's time to set a new goal for his ambition, he can then set his sights several levels higher—perhaps the executive vice presidentship. It is a justifiable ambition now because he has prepared himself for the rise, and even the presidency itself is not beyond the scope of possibilities.

However, even carefully and intelligently chosen goals and purposes are not enough. Ambition is a habit of feeling. For it to be a permanent driving force, it must be developed like every other habit is developed: through some outside stimulus, through the engagement of will power, and through repetition.

Start with your inherited instincts and tendencies. Perhaps every manager, in the beginning, tends to be ambitious to get ahead, as survival is in his nature. Laziness, comfort, overindulgence, unprofessional relationships, or other degrading elements in the office environment may block out the urge or may overrule it. The solution is to change the influence of the environment by making the office environment as advantageous as possible to the development of ambition. Counterbalance and overcome the effect of negative surroundings by placing yourself in different surroundings, if possible, or by bringing new and helpful factors into your present environment. In other words, take a strong grip on character building through willpower and habit and use them intentionally to develop ambition.

Seek opportunities to awaken the feeling of ambition. Choose responsibilities that lean toward the direction of your ambition and think about the influences which will help you achieve your goal. What must you build up systematically in preparation for ultimate victory? Have a focused purpose, keep your goal continually in mind, and have the good judgment to shut out conflicting factors. For example, common sense will dictate that your ambition to be the best manager in your department will probably be hopeless if at the same time you cultivate an ambition to be the triathlon champion. Business ambition will not survive contradictory commitment. Select your goal and stick to it faithfully.

You can stay on track with your goal more easily if you strive to express it in every thought and action. Show your ambition in the way you commence your work. The successful manager you are ambitious to be would not slight her tasks, would not waste away her time, would not scatter her attention over nonsenses. Act like the manager you wish to become, as accurately as you can, right now. Put your ambition into practice, and you will find the trait itself growing stronger and more compelling.

You can work yourself into a state of ambitiousness by dwelling on the ideal you seek to achieve, by working with your goal always in mind, and by embodying the efficiency of a top manager. For the same reason, refuse to express those thoughts and actions that are negative or opposite of the desired trait. Avoid the *don't care* and *know it all* attitudes.

The suggestive power of imitation wields enormous influence. We all have instinctive tendencies to express the same feelings we see in others, like smiling when we see others smile or crying when we see others cry. In the same way, ambition is contagious. If you associate with ambitious people, you will find yourself constantly thinking of how they succeeded and of how you may achieve the same sort of success in your career. If you read the biographies of successful business leaders, like Warren Buffet, you will find an irresistible impulse to emulate them. You will cultivate the feeling of ambition by studying the feeling of ambition; you'll find it genuinely helpful, especially in times of temporary disappointment. Stimulate your ambition by reviewing how others overcame their difficulties and achieved their planned goals.

Ambition is directly affected by the state of your physical body. The manager who is habitually the victim of poor health (i.e., obesity, chronic smoker, excessive alcohol, etc.) will not find it easy to look ahead for bigger achievements and executive positions in the business. The present is too certain and too painful to allow him to give enough thought to the future. Furthermore, the manager who has spent every night for a week gambling until one o'clock in the morning will not be able to concentrate effectively on the ambition to be the best in the organization. When physical strength is exhausted, the foundation for both mental abilities and character habits is crumbling. Therefore, keep your body physically fit. Ambition demands it.

Ambition is not certain and reliable until it has become a habit—like correct breathing and disciplined reflection. Therefore, utilize all your willpower to make the feeling of ambition into a habit. Having the desire to achieve, having selected your goal or the object of your ambition, you must put determination back of your desire and push yourself toward the realization of it.

Remember, the first and most important thing to do concerning your career is to focus your ambitions. To scatter your energy over several things means that none will get your best effort. Be ambitious. Always have a fixed mental picture of the thing you want to achieve and concentrate your effort toward its realization. It is a legitimate desire to be a successful manager in your field, so let ambition create incentive to exercise your highest talents. Put this habit into action, back it up with a steadfast purpose to achieve, and establish yourself as a driving force.

Finally, make ambition habitual. Set your mind and purpose to that one desire which is your present goal in business. Then, change that desire into a positive, constructive force by making it central and directing. Let your ambition control your theoretical weaknesses; you will be amazed at how unimportant or trivial they will show themselves to be as they disappear before focused ambition. In short, ambition will grow through use as a muscle develops with exercise.

HABIT 2

Lead with Confidence

Suppose humanity would awaken some morning to find itself grieving the loss of confidence and the world a place of chaos and inactivity. Nobody would be willing to trust to any force, agency, or promise. Trains, boats, airplanes, automobiles, and other means of transportation would stand idle; nobody would dare to risk them. Panic-stricken shareholders would overwhelm banks; nobody would be willing to trust funds to outsiders. Contracts would be broken; employees would desert their jobs; factories would close; e-commerce would close online accounts; all trade and business would cease. No manager would be willing to undertake any task of his own—self-confidence would disappear. The business world would collapse; civilization would be disrupted; starvation would press close on humanity.

It is difficult to imagine such a chaotic situation because confidence is almost common. The business world rests on confidence. Most managers have confidence in the principles of modern business. Some managers have the utmost confidence in themselves and little in other people. Some employees have confidence in people in general but suspect and doubt their employer. Other managers have no confidence in themselves; they are willing to defer to anyone's suggestion, continually stepping into the background and seldom assuming any leadership.

However, your job is to develop within yourself the habit of confidence in all its phases. As a multi-talented manager, you cannot specialize in one variety of confidence. You need to possess the habit consistently within every situation and relationship.

I have learned that *unless* you have enduring confidence within yourself, you cannot go far in business; you can never climb to any position of authority; you can never initiate anything; and you will never be a quality leader. Self-distrust and self-humiliation are fatal to real effort. Your ambition is dependent upon confidence in your ability to realize your desires. Confidence guides the habit of ambition. The confidence you have in your knowledge, skills, and abilities will impress itself upon others to respond in your favor. The manager who has no confidence in herself cannot expect others to have confidence in her. The world usually takes a manager at her self-estimation.

Self-confidence gives you an enormous advantage over the timid, hesitating manager. No manager lacking confidence can become a successful senior financial analyst. You cannot associate on an equivalent level with your colleagues or gain appreciation among the business social networks unless you have self-confidence. Once I met a shy manager who was not known within his organization, but he knew far more than any other manager. Even so, if he remains timid and fails to network within the organization, his value will remain unknown.

Not only is self-confidence essential, but the ambitious manager must have confidence in his judgment and decisions. Because confidence is the prerequisite of any decision, it is necessary to get into the habit of making decisions quickly and sticking to them. Some minds jump to conclusions and guess at results. That is not the best way to develop self-confidence or win the confidence of executives. Gather the facts and then decide.

Some minds move gradually as they gather the facts and muse over them hours or even days before forming a decision. That may appear to be the safest course of action, but in the end, it serves as a strain and bad practice. You may analyze a failure to determine its cause and its cure, but never dwell on the failure as a subject for regret. The quick decision maker may expose himself to a greater number of possible mistakes, but that risk is preferable to the alternative—always being too late for effective action.

Taking the middle ground is the wisest course of action. If you have prompt as well as sound judgment and the ability to act upon it, you have all the essentials of decisiveness. Once you have decided, stick to it. However, keep your mind open to every new fact. If you become convinced that you were wrong in your first decision, change it—do not mistake stubbornness for a strong will.

Repeated failure is often at the root of a lack of confidence. A colleague once told me that she undertook a project beyond her ability, and the disappointment over its failure destroyed her confidence. As in developing the habit of ambition, it is important to have proper judgment in developing confidence. Overconfidence is the extreme opposite of timidity, and both extremes should be avoided. The routine of being successful is the habit that builds confidence.

Having confidence in my employer and the mission of the organization is essential to honest service on my part; however, it would be very difficult to give the best that is in me to the organization if I had little faith. If I do not give my best, I am not being honest. A manager cannot (or should not) in good conscience sell or market products and services he does not have faith in. That is sound business practice—not mere sentiment. Confidence in the organization and its products and services stimulates passion, determination, commerce. Lack of confidence results in inaccuracy, distrust, and disapproval. If you have no confidence in the ability of the captain and the seaworthiness of the ship, you should not sail on it.

Confidence in others is almost as necessary as confidence in self. We cannot do our work apart from others. No successful business is ever a one-person business. Every manager is brought into daily contact with executives, colleagues, staff members under our orders, clients, customers, investors, and even solicitors—some or all of these must be met and dealt with every day. Without confidence, no sincere cooperation, no exchange of ideas, and no understanding will be found.

Lead with confidence, doing your share and then some. Realize that those under your charge will emulate a manager who is leading with confidence.

So, how can a manager develop a habit of confidence? Heredity plays a part. Some managers seem naturally confident while others tend toward hesitancy and indecision. Environment is also a factor. Managers trained at in an uplifting home and school environment step into business life with a persistent confidence; others raised in less supportive surroundings are doubtful at every turn of life, always questioning, constantly wondering, and almost never convinced about how to proceed.

Heredity and environment are in the past, and no one can change his past. However, the wise manager can control his present and plan his future. With the assistance of willpower and habit, he can directly affect his confidence (or lack of confidence) and control its future development. Confidence, like ambition, can be made a fixed habit and play a key role in developing business character.

Have faith in yourself and in your reasoning. Honestly assess your decisions, and when they have become set, back them up with a positive will.

Have confidence in your organization and be acquainted with its methods. Be so positive of its true character that you are willing to identify yourself entirely with its interests. This is an element in loyalty also, but confidence must precede loyalty.

Associate with people who possess a positive, self-confident character. By the same rule, avoid social networks of negative people and the timewasters who appear fearful of future possibilities. Opportunity to them is a trap to avoid; they risk nothing, not even their decision, and rarely achieve anything. Use your imagination and intellect to your advantage, and you will increase in confidence and reap the rewards of confidence.

As does any habit, confidence grows with repetition. Therefore, seize every opportunity to express the feeling of assurance. Be the first one to take on extra work; optimistically do any unexpected task. Your success will be its reward. In insignificant matters, as well as in the large dealings of the business, be positive and sure in your assumptions. Have confidence in your ability to be the best manager in your organization and attack every detail in your department in the same habit of confidence. You will find your confidence becoming more and more a governing emotion, more and more a motivation to action and achievement.

Be the manager of ambition and confidence. Head directly toward your goal. If obstacles are thrown in your path, leap over them. If others build a barrier in front of you, climb over it or go around. You will be stronger and more powerful for the extra effort caused by the temporary obstruction.

No one can distract you from your destiny if you are faithful to yourself and attentive to your opportunities. Confidence in yourself, confidence in your employers, and confidence in your team is a winning influence that gives double strength to ambition. Develop this power and make it a habit because it is within your reach.

Recognize your fundamental equality with the greatest managers that have lived. Refuse to be limited by thoughts others have set in motion for you. Examine yourself for the causes of your lack of success and then plan your methods of attacking them. You will win the fight by a well-thought-out system and continual action. Confidence in yourself is your principal weapon.

Enjoy your managerial duties and responsibilities; beauty and joy can be found in everything if you will look for it. I love what I do; therefore, my work is half complete before I start. Work that is disliked is only half done when it is thought to be finished. Get something out of everything, even the thing you thought would be unpleasant. Your dislike for it if is destroyed when you look for the value behind it.

A successful manager stated that he uses daily affirmations while traveling to work. He says, "I am a success. I am in power. I am the master of my destiny. Victory is mine. I know I will succeed, and nothing will be able to stop me."

The Statue of Liberty, located in New York harbor, is one of the most impressive sights found in the United States. Her calm graciousness is the result of perfect physical poise and steady strength. In her uplifted hand, she holds the signal of her office, the light which only liberty can throw into the dark places of the world. In the goodness of her manner, we see the reflection of not only political and economic freedom but also freedom of mind and thought.

If you sincerely desire to be a successful manager, let the Statue of Liberty inspire you as she inspires the immigrant. To him, she means leaving behind the old methods of government and unjust laws. She tells him every person has value and promises success and freedom of opportunity for everyone. Embrace the promise of success and opportunity for yourself.

You have been bound and limited by the thoughts others have formulated for you. Yet, thoughts of not being good enough, not being of smart enough, and not being the right fit will erode your confidence. Leave these negative thoughts behind because they are not for you. Say aloud, "I will succeed. As I take on new challenges, I feel calm, confident, and powerful." Such thoughts as these, firmly held, will bring quiet dignity and conscious strength and will grow into a conviction that you mean what you say.

Self-confidence means the difference between a restricted and a developed personality. Over and over, tell yourself that you have no fear, are destined for success, and will not acknowledge obstacles. Again, the routine of being successful is the habit that builds confidence.

HABIT 3

Display Loyalty

Any successful team, whether sports, business, medical, or scientific, demands loyalty. Staff cannot work together successfully in any organization or for any cause unless loyalty is among them—the loyalty of everyone to the team. The great athletes Larry Bird and Michael Jordan (not related but I wish) played for NBA teams, the Boston Celtics and Chicago Bulls respectively. Wisely, they subordinated their individual magnificence to their loyalty to their team. Likewise, in every kind of teamwork, individual interests are secondary. The interests of the team are dominant, demanding unwavering loyalty from every member.

Most twenty-first-century organizations promote complete and efficient teamwork. The hospital is a team. The department store is a team. The bank is a team. Business establishments of every kind are teams organized to produce products or services through cooperative work. For this reason, loyalty is a fundamental and essential habit in the make-up of business character. Without loyalty, teamwork wouldn't work; without teamwork, millennial businesses would fall to pieces.

The first obligation of every manager in business is to be loyal to the business, organization, or company that employs him. Without loyalty, he cannot be effective. Whether his work is that of operations manager, quality control manager, office manager, or receptionist, he cannot be 100 percent productive unless he is loyal, committed to the work, and has truly identified his interests with those of his employer. Half-hearted loyalty in business is just as damaging to productivity as half-hearted commitment to an athletic team or the Navy.

The manager who works by watching the clock, doing just as little within the required time as she possibly can, is not loyal either to her own interests or those of her employer. The careless purchasing manager, who spends the company's money regardless of the economy, is not loyal. The sales manager who calls his selling dialog "small talk" and explains to his associates that he is just hanging on to the job until he can find something better, is not loyal. No manager can qualify as loyal if he casually assumes his business duties and responsibilities while continuously looking for a new job. He has not considered his permanent connection to the organization and gives as little effort to his work as he possibly can.

Knowledge, skills, and abilities—none of these desirable job qualifications can overcome disloyalty. It destroys every good element in the business character of the manager who engages in it and likely erodes the larger enterprise.

But bear in mind, loyalty is not a habit that can be cultivated in the expectation of gaining profit or reward. The very core of loyalty is unselfishness. To be faithful to the organization in an emergency because you suspect you may gain by it is not loyalty. Devotion inspired by the fear of discovery is not loyalty. Faithfulness to an organization or a cause because it is *your* organization or *your* cause is loyalty. Loyalty unmixed with expectation of personal profit is true loyalty. It is a habit that steadies ambition and provides a solid foundation for all personal relationships. It is the only kind of loyalty worth having. Anything other than this is selfishness disguised as loyalty.

Your loyalty should express itself in steady faithfulness to the organization in times of seeming disaster and emergency as well as in everyday routine. This is the kind of loyalty that cements and holds in the minds of executives. Generally, the loyal manager receives fair treatment because it is human nature to return loyalty for loyalty. Self-respect and proper regard for integrity compel the employer to deal fairly with the manager who expresses in all his feelings and actions an unfaltering loyalty to the organization. The team must be loyal to the individual as well as the individual to the team.

How can you develop loyalty as a dominant habit in your business character? You already possess a natural tendency to loyalty. As children, we are passionately loyal to parents and teachers. We defend our political candidate against every suspicion; we hold to our religion despite the critics; we are passionately loyal to our country. It is widely known that Donald J. Trump, the forty-fifth president of the United States, rewarded and respected loyalty while in business and the presidency.

Developing the habit is a matter of exercising and directing loyalty until it becomes established in character as a consistent habit of feeling. The basis of its development is confidence and awareness.

No manager can truly be loyal to any organization in which he has little interest or of which he is suspicious. The sailor who doubts the integrity of his cause cannot provide good service. The athlete who believes favoritism rules the coaches and leader of his team cannot play the most effective soccer. Likewise, on the business team, you must have confidence in your team, its leaders, and its work. You must be genuinely interested in its mission and vision.

The first step is to cultivate an intelligent interest in your organization and recognize your part in it. See yourself not as an isolated individual only working for a salary but as a team member working to produce the best products or the most efficient service of which that organization is capable. In other words, recognize that, as a part of the business team, your efforts contribute to your company's success and the better you do your work, the more effective and successful the team will be. Possessing such an attitude in business is essential to positive thinking and is a prerequisite to loyalty.

Overconfidence and uncontrolled ambition are two exaggerations that must be avoided as they lead to disloyalty. The manager whose ambition becomes an obsession, urging her to seek promotion beyond her capability, is foredoomed to failure. Failure leads to criticism, and criticism is not the atmosphere that stimulates loyalty. Overconfidence is like uncontrolled ambition—the manager who has one is likely to have the other. Do not rate your abilities or your importance too high. Do not expect to elbow your way to success. Keep a proper balance of confidence and humility; it will help your loyalty.

Utilize your inherent tendency to be loyal, to select the right side, and to fight for your side. Do not apologize to yourself for loyalty; rather let loyalty express itself freely. Be proud of your organization, proud of its reputation and success, proud that you are a part of its legacy. Repeatedly show your loyalty through actions, not just in talking about it.

Make your present environment stimulating to loyalty by shunning the pessimistic and negative. Instead, foster association with the most loyal person in your organization. Talk to them. Get their point of view. It will stimulate both your interest and your confidence, and the habit of loyalty you see in others will inevitably become expressed within you.

On the flip side, you will discover the inevitable "hater" in every office or shop or store. His criticisms are destructive to loyalty—unless you shut him out. You can exclude him from your mind if you ignore him.

Finally, make loyalty a habit. This means engaging your willpower in every possible way to stimulate loyalty whenever the opportunity arises. Practice loyalty by applying it consistently as a guiding principle to the business character.

Loyalty, to be effective, must become a consistent, constant habit of character. Everyday loyalty, loyalty in routine effort as well as in the time of excitement and loyalty in little things as well as in big things, is the loyalty that bolsters business relations. It makes it possible to delegate responsibility, which makes teamwork more efficient.

Loyalty is a necessary element in business character. If you have been recognized in your organization or climbed to places of higher responsibility or leadership, you have loyalty. Loyalty binds your faithfulness and abilities together in a stronger combination for company service, and it ties you ever closer to the mission and vision of the organization, your team, and your colleagues.

HABIT 4

Know What You're Passionate About

Most successful managers started with knowledge, skills, and abilities, but these only carried them but so far until they were inspired by passion. Passion transforms everyday effort into a fascinating game. It motivates and quickens, transforming the routine manager into the enthusiastic manager.

Nothing great was ever achieved without passion. It has marked the leader and the successful innovator in every generation. Passion was as indispensable to the voyage of Christopher Columbus as the trade winds that pushed his ship across the Atlantic Ocean. Passion for liberty produced the Declaration of Independence and the freedom of the American Colonies. Passion planted the seeds of the Civil Rights movement and landed the space shuttle on the moon. Passion brought us from the Industrial Age into the Technological Age.

Without passion, the marketing manager's promotion and sales campaign would dissipate; the shipping and receiving manager would not receive incoming material; the forward press of business would slack into a snail's pace. Passion transforms a task and overcomes the obstacles.

Passion is a personal quality. The passion for a sales campaign is simply the sum of the separate passions of the individuals on the marketing manager's team. The passion of a large organization does not exist apart from the personnel who make up the organization and represent it. Passion is personal and individual. We generate it within ourselves.

Additionally, passion is a highly contagious quality. The successful manager spreads passion wherever he goes. The passionate purchasing manager wins new customers and continually strengthens his standing with the old ones. One manager was so passionate that she became very popular and the most successful in her organization. Another successful manager said that if he failed to give his team a strong dose of passion on Monday, the volume of business dropped the following week. The passionate manager can write a more effective business letter, negotiate a better contract, and represent the organization more successfully in any situation than the manager who lacks the overwhelming power of passion.

It is just as necessary for the receptionist to put passion into her work as it is for the highest executive. The Human Resources manager who is passionate is likely to be loyal and ambitious as well as time saving and energetic. The passionate real estate portfolio manager will never be the one to forget responsibility in the boredom of routine work. The passionate automotive manager will make fewer mistakes and will more quickly become a trained and skilled operative. Bottom line: successful managers do not spare themselves in doing their share. There is no department and no position where passion will not count positively and favorably. It is a business asset, an important factor in success, and an essential element in the character of all managers.

And passion can be acquired. Even the manager with a miserable nature can form the habit of passion. The development of this habit is largely a matter of environment and willpower.

Since passion grows from interest, no one can become passionate about baseball until he knows the game and has developed an interest in it. A colleague took his family on vacation to Orlando, visited Disney World and Legoland, and returned home passionate about that magic, scenic wonderland. Why? Because he had developed an interest in it. Before his trip, he knew little of Disney World and had no interest in it. The moment he developed the interest, he discovered that he was passionate. Now, it has become an annual vacation spot.

Likewise, if you want to become passionate about the healthcare business, get acquainted with it and develop an interest in it. If you would be passionate about cybersecurity, learn all that you can about its origin, methods, and products. When you develop an interest, it can grow into a passion.

In developing the habit of passion, the first step is to get thoroughly acquainted with your organization. This will give you not only interest but also confidence, another essential element in passion. It helps you to know what you are passionate about. The so-called passion of the doubter, the pessimist, or questioner, who still feels that he must *boost himself above others*, is not true passion. Quality managers can feel when passion is not genuine. There is a powerful substance as the foundation in passion, which may not be confidence. Have confidence in yourself, in your organization, and in your team; then, you have a foundation for passion.

Second, you must exercise passion. Give passion free play; do not suppress it; do not be ashamed of it; it needs no apology. Give it a chance to express itself through exercise so that it may develop into a habit. Bring imagination into action as an aid to passion. Successful managers possess the imagination to see the possibilities of their situation, the future success of their careers, and the importance of their organization. Once they place themselves in an atmosphere or environment of passion, they cannot help but feel the emotional impulse of their surroundings.

A successful manager can make colleagues passionate simply by being alive with passion. His colleagues will emulate him by getting into the spirit of their associate. The instinct to emulate is effective. Moreover, the manager develops strength in his passion as he exercises it. He may be somewhat passionate the first week but totally passionate and thoroughly infused at the end of a few weeks—passion has then become a habit.

Third, utilize association by seeking the company of successful, optimistic, and ambitious managers. Read books that will offer new perspectives; converse with those who can give you significant points of view that are helpful and stimulating.

Fourth, express passion in your body language. Hold your head up and your shoulders back. Walk briskly and breathe deeply. It will inspire your purpose, strengthen your resources, quicken your energies, and help you to achieve your goals.

"Our manager has exercised so much passion that we exceeded sales by 80 percent—that's why we have been succeeding for several weeks now," said a supervisor of a large retail store. This manager has succeeded in infusing into members of his team his habit of passion. Emulation of his energy and personality have caused passion to permeate throughout his entire staff of employees.

Passion is the propelling force necessary for climbing the business ladder of success.

HABIT 5

Think Optimistically

I recently read a story about how a successful managing editor named Lee was thrown from a motorcycle years ago. Three joints in his backbone were crushed, his spine was severed, and his left arm, right leg, collarbone, and three ribs were broken. For a while, he floated between life and death. Finally, it was determined that he would live, though he would suffer paralysis from his hips down, condemned to lie on his back for the rest of his life.

However, he never displayed an attitude of pessimism or discouragement. Despite his physical limitations, he conducted business, edited a paper, and was a constant distributer of optimism. He invented a stand for his laptop so he could handle all correspondence in bed. Though he suffered constant pain, he still maintained a bright temperament and was the source of encouragement for hundreds of men and women who read his writings. No one who visited him failed to see in him a bright promise. They learned that even the darkest disaster could not obscure the joy of living and achieving in the person who sees life through the lens of optimism.

All managers can learn from Lee and adopt an optimistic disposition, even under the most discouraging conditions. Managers have no excuse to complain all the time. Worry, fear, and hopelessness are mental states. They do not own us without our consent. They cannot grow unless we allow them and nurture them. The deliberate practice of thinking optimistically is the one effective antidote to all those negative emotions, and thinking optimistically is possible in every manager.

The successful manager possesses the habit of optimism. Mean humor, a bad temper, and unhappiness are all abnormal states, conditions which destroy optimism and eliminate positivity from your character. Likewise, selfishness detracts from optimism. The extremely selfish manager cannot be optimistic simply because he thinks only of his interests and comfort instead of those of others. Optimism is based on sympathy, but the selfish manager has no sympathy. He cannot look at a situation from the viewpoint of his organization or his team. His understanding is limited to his own narrowed vision, and his attitude toward others is primarily one of distrust and criticism.

The selfish manager is impatient and easily becomes irritable. Watch him at the telephone, watch him doing business with a dissatisfied customer, and watch him in any of the large or small emergencies of business. He becomes a chronic faultfinder. His associates label him as a complainer and avoid him. He may keep his job, but that is all he will have. If he achieves success, his character is such that he will hardly appreciate it.

Fear is another condition that destroys optimism. Are you frightened of losing your job or position? Do you fear consequences of past deeds or that you will not meet a project deadline? Sadly, you are carrying a loathsome burden. Optimism cannot exist with fear because fear leads to worry, and worries poison the mind and smother all healthy habits of character.

The original meaning of the word *worry* was "a choke." This definition still holds today. Worry chokes ambition, chokes confidence, chokes loyalty, chokes passion, and most of all, it chokes optimism. The miserable manager who moves about as though she were under a cloud, who casts gloom wherever she goes, is the victim of fear.

Lock out selfishness and fear, and optimism intuitively grows within. Thinking optimistically is agreeable; it is beneficial; and it attracts. Selfishness and fear are negative; they destroy and repel. Negative qualities cannot exist with the positive as darkness cannot exist with light.

Happy and healthy settings stimulate optimistic thinking. Cleanliness, sunshine, crisp air, lively music, and bright colors all inspire optimism. The optimistic manager attracts business and friends; he ties himself to them with words of sympathy and common understanding. He attracts the confidence and respect of others, ultimately attracting larger responsibilities and upward mobility in his career. The organization that is filled with optimism, where smiles, courtesy, and manners are the rule and not the exception, is the company that becomes popular—it attracts.

Several years ago, on Christmas Eve, Gregory Collins, a Navy officer, walked into a shoe store and asked for a pair of penny loafers.

"Downstairs," said the salesperson. Downstairs he went.

In the store, several employees were standing around conversing and on their cell phones. It was a rainy day, and few customers were out. No one paid any attention to Greg as he walked slowly to the rear where the penny loafers were displayed. After a while, a salesperson detached himself from the others and strolled over to Greg.

"Something you want?" he asked. Greg explained that he had come to purchase a pair of penny loafers.

"Well, there they are," and the salesperson as he pointed to the shoes. His style was as cold and dreary as the weather outside.

"What is the price?" Greg asked, picking up a pair.

"Ninety-five dollars and ninety-nine cents," came the answer.

Greg said, "Do you have any penny loafers for around seventy dollars?"

The salesperson pointed to a pair of loafers on the top shelf. "Those are sixty-nine dollars and ninety-nine cents," he said and stood uselessly waiting, bored attitude apparent. He made no effort to get the shoes down for Greg and had no interest in selling. Therefore, Greg left the store.

Into another store Greg went. A sales representative approached him immediately. His smile dismissed the gloom of the weather, and his optimism was contagious. He offered various styles of loafers and volunteered information as to the inherent value of each. After a style had been selected, the sales representative searched through the stock until Greg was satisfied that no other pair would suit him better. Finally, two pairs of penny loafers were purchased. As Greg was leaving, the sales representative said, "We wish you a Merry Christmas, sir, and if you have any issues whatsoever with the loafers, bring them back after Christmas, and we'll change them or refund your money. It's been a pleasure serving you."

Which of these sales representatives would you keep on your team? One had sympathy and understanding. He put cheerfulness into his service, infused optimism into his selling, and made a new friend for the store. The other sales representative was selfish and self-centered, treating the customer as an intruder. The selfish sales representative probably did not mean to be rude, but it was his nature and part of his character.

The difference between those two sales representatives is simply a difference in habits of character. The coldness was part of the nature of the unprofessional sales representative simply because he had cultivated and developed the habit of selfishness for most of his life. Thinking optimistically was in the nature of the professional sales representative because he had cultivated optimism. He made it a point to please other people, to do the thing he would want done were he in the customer's shoes (no pun intended).

It is not sporadic optimism that counts but the consistent tendency to see the bright side. Thinking optimistically must become a habit. The habit of optimism is formed, as habits of pessimism are formed, by repetition.

You must develop the habit of optimism by looking for the bright side of things, even when you are tempted to dwell on dark and depressing circumstances. Every environment contains elements that lead to optimism and others that lead to pessimism. Therefore, you must use the power of choice to focus on some essentials of your environment while disregarding others. Think about the advantages of your duties and responsibilities and be optimistic, or you may dwell on disadvantages and be disappointed and unappreciative.

Thinking optimistically is not automatically attached to any type of organization. It may be absent from the Fortune 500 company but alive and effective in the Fortune 100 company. It is all a matter of willpower and habit, using willpower to close out the discouraging influences and make thinking optimistically habitual.

Improve the habit of optimism by looking at things from other people's point of view. Develop sympathy by striving to understand others deeply, with the aim to provide efficient, individualized service. For example, the sales representative should direct his selling activities from the customer's point of view. Sympathy breeds optimism, which limits complications in human relations in business: customer to store, employee to employer, or team to manager. When thinking optimistically, one possesses sympathy, which assists in illuminating and simplifying the situation.

To be a successful manager, you must associate with optimistic people. Of course, you may help those who are in distress but do not emulate their behaviors of feeling. Let your optimistic thinking lead the situation; let it help and strengthen you. As much as possible, be in the social networks of optimists. I like to read books that view life as full of promise, and I stay clear of gloomy, depressing books. Thinking optimistically is constructive, natural, and healthy.

Commit yourself to a pleasant day by saying, "Good-morning," whether you feel happy or not. If you repeatedly think optimistically and cheerfully, you will become optimistic.

As a manager, strengthen your desire for thinking optimistically by exercising your will. Require yourself to put this decision into practice. Use your willpower. Drive your purpose into action. Each separate victory will strengthen your purpose into a habit and guide optimism into your very nature.

HABIT 6

Be Consistent

Three attributes identify the consistent manager: honesty, punctuality, and meticulousness. Without this trinity, no real productivity can be achieved in business. No matter how brilliant a manager might be, if he is dishonest or habitually late or insincere in his work, he is destined to failure. He lacks the foundation of honor, the bedrock upon which good character must be built.

Honesty means more than simply keeping within the regulations and policies. No manager need brag because he has never stolen from the organization or been in danger of prosecution for embezzling. Honesty examines a manager's nature and tests his motives. It queries his purposes and decisions, which guide his action in small things as well as large ones.

The office manager who takes an occasional highlighter from the desk drawer and uses it for her purpose is stealing. Of course, it will not break the organization and may never be missed. However, the office manager who takes a stamp is doing on a small scale the same sort of thing that a bank teller does who steals a stack of fifty-dollar bills. She is taking advantage of her position to gain a personal return. She is betraying the trust given to her and imposing a prodigious loss on herself.

If you are a manager who wastes time in your office, you are wasting money, for time is money. The time you waste is the organization's time, and you have agreed to sell your knowledge, skills, and abilities for eight hours a day for a nice annual salary. So, then, why waste even twenty minutes of it each day by malingering or gossiping or any of the other time-destroying pastimes?

Honesty means exhaustive integrity, which is strict accountability in all your actions. It is a principle of conduct, and no exceptions are made to the principle. The rule is straight and unchanging; it measures all things alike with these searching questions: Is this right? Is it factual? Is it mine?

The prompt manager is the on-time manager. If the meeting is scheduled for five o'clock, he is there exactly five minutes early. If the office opens at eight thirty, he is at his desk at 8:55 a.m. to start working at nine. If an assigned task is to be finished within three hours, he gets the job done in two hours and thirty minutes. As far as it relates to wasting time, promptness includes the component of honesty. The manager who comes drifting in at nine o'clock is not punctual; he has already failed.

The most serious and immediate consequence of tardiness is the effect upon other people whose work is delayed or whose system is disrupted by the carelessness of the irresponsible manager. It also effects the character of the manager, giving him a reputation for irregularity that is difficult to live down. The on-time manager is well-organized and more likely to get positive attention than the one who is careless. He utilizes his time to obtain results.

Meticulousness goes hand in hand with honesty. No honest manager can hold back on a task. He knows it is not right, the work will not stand, and the result is not final. Meticulousness costs time and effort, but successful managers know it is time and effort well spent. And, taking the long view, it is cheapest to do it correctly from the start.

"It's good enough" is the expression of the insincere manager, hurrying through one job with his mind already on the next one. Nothing is *good enough* until it is as good as it should be. The temporary can never replace the carefully formed result—whether it be an achievement in the shop, office, or boardroom.

You must possess consistency in its threefold form: you must be honest; you must be punctual; you must be meticulousness. You must also be reliable in each. How does a manager develop the habit?

Company culture is a powerful factor. Even the most careful, punctual, and exact manager will fall into careless habits if he is regularly associated with people who are careless and irresponsible. It is easy to drift into pessimistic ways of thinking and doing. Every careless act, every broken promise, and every neglected requirement ensures the habit of inconsistency and lowers the manager's standards of conduct. On the other hand, association with people who are aware of the finer points of honor, who never make a false promise or a bogus excuse, and who are careful and meticulous in their work will be a positive help to the strengthening of consistency.

Therefore, utilize this assistance and associate with people of consistency. You select your associates, so choose those who are truthful, careful, and faithful in the tasks entrusted to them. This will require the exercise of your willpower and power of decision and choice. Nevertheless, the tendency to emulate is so natural that no genuinely ambitious manager can afford to risk the contagion that a continuous example of inconsistency threatens.

Your actions must be examined and guided by pure motives. You may have heard the doctrine, honesty is the best policy. I do believe you must be honest regardless of the consequences. Honesty due to fear of exposure and reprimand is a poor motive. You must be honest with yourself first.

The best motives for honesty are self-respect, high ideals, and worthy friends. Develop self-respect, and it will save you from careless ways. Seek high ideals, and they will keep you persistent. Develop friendships that are well-intentioned and caring because they will reinforce your self-respect and strengthen your purpose.

No matter how inspiring and supportive the atmosphere may be, convenience, personal advantage, or comfort may sometimes suggest that you relax your rule by telling a white lie, "forgetting" the meeting, or hurrying through a task sloppily. To submit to such suggestions is to weaken your attribute of consistency. Keep to the committed course and do not allow exceptions. Hold yourself to the standard and seek to make consistency habitual.

Habits are formed and strengthened by repetition. Repeat the thought and the act with no exception and no break in the chain. If an unavoidable emergency does interrupt your schedule and you are delayed for a meeting or late in completing a project, penalize yourself. Force yourself to reach the office half an hour earlier the next day to make up for the lost time. Take pride in the mastery of yourself. When you give yourself a task, do not give up until it is complete. The technology manager who resolves to test a new, innovative method should force himself to see the test through, even though it may prove exasperating.

Invincible determination (Habit 8) is a mighty helper in establishing habits of consistency.

Extravagant claims, cut-price deception, and dishonest advertising may attract business for a while, but reality will inevitably come. Take any of the large chain stores that have become public institutions in their communities—Wal-Mart, Target, Costco, and Sam's Club, for example—and you will find that their success is based on their unfailing reputation for honesty and fairness. The public has labeled them *consistent* and, therefore, trusts them, depends on them, and supports them.

The manager who is recognized and sought after in business is consistent. Those who seek his services have confidence in him, and they buy his products. In turn, he is promoted to greater responsibilities and a larger salary because they have confidence in him. The consistent manger moves ahead. Without consistency, ambition is just an instant ride to a bad fall. Without consistency, confidence rests on unstable ground; real loyalty is impossible; passion is simple fizz; and optimism can be little more than pretense and deception.

Being consistent is a fundamental character trait. You are not seeking a momentary advantage but to be a successful manager over your entire career. You need to make the habit of consistency the very foundation of your character. You can neither build securely nor succeed in any relationship without it. You cannot profit long-term in any business without it. The successful manager is consistently truthful and fair, on time, and faithful to his organization. He is the forward-moving manager, the ultimate leader, and the go-getter in every business.

HABIT 7

Get-Up-and-Go!

I n 1880, an eighteen-year-old youth gave up his job as driver of a stagecoach in interior Pennsylvania to become a clerk in a grocery store at Braddock. He slept in the store and was at work from six thirty in the morning until ten thirty every night. In odd moments he could spare from work, he studied mathematics.

Braddock was the seat of the Edgar Thomson Steel Company's plant, and the steelworkers comprised the bulk of the customers for the store. The grocery boy took an eager interest in the big plant. He began to study the development of the iron industry, and it was not long before he decided more opportunity could be found for his energies in steel than in groceries. One evening Captain Bill Jones, manager of the Edgar Thomson works, called at the store to make a purchase, and the ambitious clerk asked him for a job.

"Sure, I can give you a job," said Captain Bill. "You can start driving stakes and carrying chains for the engineers. The pay is a dollar a day." Therefore, Charles M. Schwab entered the steel business.

Driving stakes and carrying chains is wearying work, but young Schwab leaped to the opportunity. He worked with all his energies during the day, and at night he pored over books on mechanics and engineering, seeking to prepare himself for more important tasks. Within six months, the chain-carrier was made assistant engineer. From that, he climbed to the position of engineer, and at the end of three years, he oversaw the entire engineering corps.

This ex-grocery clerk had now become Captain Bill's right-hand man. He built eight gigantic blast furnaces at the Edgar Thomson plant, and steel men throughout the country sat up and took notice. Then he designed the great Homestead steel plant and built it. When the plant was finished, Andrew Carnegie placed young Schwab in charge of it and made him a partner in the Carnegie organization. He was only seven years removed from the town grocery store, but during that time, the marvelous *get-up-and-go* of this man had formed miracles. It had made him master of the details of steel manufacture as few men have been, and it strengthened his character traits in countless ways that make for leadership.

Mr. Carnegie recognized him as a leader and made him president of the Carnegie Steel Company. When JP Morgan and his associates bought out Carnegie and other steel companies and merged them to form the billion-dollar United States Steel Corporation, they made Charles M. Schwab the president of the vast organization.

Schwab personifies get-up-and-go. The phrase "human livewire" has been misused in many cases, but it literally applies to Schwab. He was a livewire, a producer of get-up-and-go, a mighty generator of those powers of mind and spirit which drive men on to labor, which keep them at difficult and uncongenial tasks in spite of distractions and allurements. His great get-up-and-go carried him over many an insurmountable obstacle; it compelled him to undertake big tasks and tackle the most difficult problems. It made him ambitious for the highest achievement.

When the steel king resigned from the presidency of the United States Steel Corporation, people said, "Schwab has made his pile and quit." The fact is, he was looking ahead to his biggest task and his greatest industrial achievement. The Bethlehem Steel Company, of which he had acquired control, was known as the graveyard of many fortunes; its plant had degenerated into a rusty aggregation of dilapidated machinery; its business had sunk to the minimum; nothing seemed to be ahead but failure. Schwab, who was rich enough to retire and enjoy his wealth, set himself to the laborious work of revitalizing and rebuilding that dying industry.

In 1916, Bethlehem Steel Company was one of the most noticeable steel manufacturers in the world, occupying more than thirteen hundred acres. It had busy rolling mills, shops, and furnaces, employing more than sixty thousand men, and the enormous plant was working day and night to peak capacity. When his task had been accomplished, Mr. Schwab said to a correspondent of *The American Magazine*:

> I always pity the man who says, "When I get so much money, I am going to retire and enjoy life." The greatest thrill that can come to any man is the thrill of successful accomplishment. In the last year, I have had the opportunity to sell out Bethlehem for almost fabulous sums. They did not even interest me. If I gave up my business, I would be resigning my greatest interest in life.

Get-up-and-go is powerful, moving energy and was the secret of Charles M. Schwab's success. When he assumed control of Bethlehem Steel, he went to work. For three years, he punched the time clock as often and devotedly as the routine worker in his plant. From seven in the morning to eight at night, he was at the plant. Wherever he went, he displayed and communicated his habits of character. His ambition was contagious, and his team worked hard for long hours to make Bethlehem successful. They had confidence in him, and he in them. His optimism and passion reinforced confidence. His consistency proved it. His energy demonstrated it through get-up-and-go!

The energy of the body and mind is energy that dominates and triggers the entire person. Get-up-and-go was the central habit in the character of Charles M. Schwab. He became a successful manager and executive because he was willing to work for it. After more than a hundred years, we appreciate his significance as a symbol of what any man can do through substantial effort. Schwab set an example of how to walk up the hard steps of experience, one at a time, to a place of wealth and power.

All his life, Charles M. Schwab was a worker. No man in his steel mills ever worked harder or more persistently than the owner himself. Moreover, from his work came the rewards, the natural fruits of get-up-and-go, and the inevitable results of energy wisely directed and accurately applied.

Today, in so many other cases, we observe successful managers utilizing get-up-and-go as their working, winning quality. A manager may have ambition, confidence, loyalty, passion, and other habits of character, but if he is without the energy of get-up-and-go, he will remain unsuccessful. The timewasting manager is not the energetic type with the get-up-and-go dynamic quality. This character trait goes forward and acts. Get-up-and-go utilizes confidence, loyalty, passion, and optimism but then pushes ahead to the achievement of ambition. It goes hand in hand with consistency. No manager can be consistent who is lazy and lethargic. Invincible determination, initiative, and self-control are each dependent on get-up-and-go. They are but mere concepts unless they are activated by the habit which stimulates business and prompts a manager to work.

This work habit, get-up-and-go, is within the reach of every manager striving for success. Some managers appear to be born lazy, but by the exercise of willpower, habits of get-up-and-go can be substituted for habits of laziness. No nature is so inactive and lethargically inclined that it cannot be recharged and revitalized under habits of purposeful work.

One of the strong controlling factors in the development of get-up-and-go as a character habit is health. Managers who place themselves in a condition of physical fitness will immediately find a quickening of their get-up and-go. Fatigue, lack of sleep, lack of recreation, headache and other pains, an excess of unhealthy foods or alcohol—all these are abnormal conditions of the physical machine and destructive to get-up-and-go. They undermine the very foundation of get-up-and-go— physical strength—and their influence on the mind is depressive and discouraging. Good health is a prerequisite to the development of normal get-up-and-go.

Therefore, your first aid to the development of get-up-and-go is health. Focused habits of exercise, correct habits of eating and working, and correct habits of recreation—these form the best basis for the development of the true habit of get-up-and-go. Without them, it is practically impossible to bring or keep your energies up to peak proficiency.

The energetic manager transfers his habit to his team. Let us not forget Charles M. Schwab's example. He personified a successful manager of get-up-and-go and transferred his passion to his employees. A successful manager will frequently have a more motivating effect on a lazy team member than countless words of threat or discipline. And the opposite is true as well; a successful manager surrounded by timewasters is likely to fall into lazy habits. It is only by the exercise of willpower that he can keep himself strong against negative influence or habits.

Your second aid to the development of get-up-and-go, then, is environment. Seek the camaraderie of people who are attentive, enthusiastic, and sincerely dynamic in their work. Business obligations may fling you in direct contact with lazy staff members who add no value, but your willpower can minimize their influence. However, you must keep yourself to your normal get-up-and-go by looking ahead to your goals, by keeping alive all your interest in your duties and responsibilities, and by selecting associates who possess get-up-and-go and its complementary behaviors.

The habits of ambition, confidence, passion, optimism, and consistency are powerful stimulants of get-up-and-go. All courteous feelings tend to develop get-up-and-go. The ambitious manager must become a manager of get-up-and-go; or else, his ambition will be weak and uncertain.

The manager of confidence is excited to move forward and act. Passion and optimism feed get-up-and-go, urging it on to larger efforts. Initiative and invincible determination must have the cooperation of get-up-and-go, or else they are no more than a desire or an inclination. Without get-up-and-go, self-control can be nothing more than an nice thought.

Your third aid to the development of get-up-and-go is the growth of the other character habits. If you round out your character in the other habits, you will find the impulse to act and achieve becomes stronger and more powerful. Your get-up-and-go will grow with your character development.

Your fourth and all-important aid is willpower. Willpower is the necessary co-worker with each of the previous aids. For without willpower, you cannot control your health; without willpower, you cannot affect your environment; without willpower, you cannot call to your aid any of the other character habits. Without willpower, you cannot make get-up-and-go a controlling habit of your career—or life.

With willpower, you can work miracles in the development of your character. Willpower can carry you over the difficulties of a bad start; it can neutralize a negative environment; it can substitute good habits for bad habits.

Willpower will overcome the negative effects of over caution, ridicule, and fear of failure. It will substitute a positive, assertive attitude for the attitude of *don't care*. It will develop an interest in work and make you strong enough to turn away from all influences that weaken get-up-and-go. It will give you the power to establish get-up-and-go as a consistent habit of action.

Laziness may seem to be an inherited quality, but willpower can overcome laziness. Get-up-and-go may seem to be a gift given to a few favored individuals, but willpower can develop it in any manager. With willpower, you can develop the necessary work power within you. Also, work power is the power that achieves, the power that accomplishes results.

Nathaniel Bowditch is an American mathematician remembered and often credited as the founder of modern maritime navigation. His book *The New American Practical Navigator* (1802) is still carried on board every commissioned US Naval vessel today. Bowditch once said to a young man, "Never undertake anything but with the feeling that you can and will do it."

Isaac Rich, an example of get-up-and-go and invincible determination, was residing on Cape Cod when he decided to set out to find his wealth in Boston. He was optimistic, adventurous, and candid; and he knew enough about maritime life to start his life there. He saw a better opportunity in the capital of Boston and committed to trying there without any assistance. He had no job in mind but was prepared to accept any decent position that might be offered.

So, he traveled to Boston with only a few dollars in his pocket. Once he reached the city, he began searching immediately to find a job; and he traveled and traveled, applying in vain for jobs and finding none.

After each rejection, Rich was strongly tempted to return home, but his determined heart rose in rebellion against the thought. He would not return embarrassed. His get-up-and-go said, "If I can't find a situation, I will make one."

Rich found a wooden board and transformed it into an oyster stand on the corner of a street. He borrowed a wheelbarrow and walked three miles to an oyster cuff, where he purchased three bushels of the bivalves and wheeled them to his place of business. He was now a Boston merchant, made so by circumstances that at first seemed hopeless.

Rich sold all his oysters on the first day and was extremely satisfied with his profits. He continued this method of doing business until he had earned hundreds of dollars, with which he purchased transportation. He moved his place of business from outdoors into a rented room.

Rich continued to grow his business rapidly and soon leased the entire building, creating departments and adding to his property. He became a successful manager, executive, and Boston millionaire. He donated large portions of his money, leaving hundreds of thousands at his death to found Boston University, where young men and women are educated to this day.

Decision is more of the head; get-up-and-go is more of the heart. The latter is the power to produce positive effects. It is recorded of Hezekiah in the Bible, "And in every work that he began in the service of the house of God, in the law and in the commandment, to seek his God, he did *it* with all his heart, so he prospered," 2 Chronicles 31:21, NKJV.

"With all the heart" is Hezekiah's energy, his get-up-and-go. Without it, no one prospers in anything. Success comes to the class of managers who pursue their life work "with all the heart."

The motto of successful managers is well expressed as, "I will find a way or make it."

HABIT 8

Act with Invincible Determination

On a quiet street in a secluded sector of New York City stood a twelve-story building devoted to original scientific research. A group of experts worked there tackling difficult scientific problems and pursuing them to conclusion. Whether a problem in electricity, or a mystery in chemistry, or a difficulty in engineering, the issue was never abandoned until its questions were answered. Even if it required six days or six years, they never gave up until every uncertain element or undetermined factor in the situation was explored, tested, and concluded.

One habit is dominant in the character of those who work in laboratories: invincible determination. Discouragement is nothing; distractions never distract; impossibility is an unknown word. The desired result is targeted as a destination to be reached, and it usually is attained. Invincible determination is the policy of ceaselessly keeping at it, which makes achievement the rule and failure the rare exception.

Invincible determination is the staying power that keeps drive resolute, get-up-and-go at its task, and ambition active. Alexander Graham Bell determined that electricity could be made to transmit the human voice over a wire; Thomas Edison determined that lightning could be created, controlled, and used to light cities; Cyrus H. McCormick determined that a machine could harvest grain and replace hundreds of manual workers. It was long and exhausting work for these men before satisfactory results rewarded them. Each performed several experiments and failed repeatedly. Yet they held on to their purpose, stayed with the task, tried again, and finally won.

Everywhere in business, whether the shop, the store, the office, the boardroom, or on the road, the determined manager is the manager who overcomes. For one thing, the manager of invincible determination is commonly a manager of get-up-and-go, consistency, loyalty, and confidence. These powerful habits of character reinforce him, and as he strengthens his habit of invincible determination, he strengthens his other habits. The financial manager who will not give up the search for an elusive item until she finds it—dinner or no dinner—is the staff member who will stay in any emergency, big or small. She will continue her task until it is accomplished. Any business management position requires the application of invincible determination, which is an essential element of staying power—and only the stayer can consistently succeed.

I know a determined manager who *hates to be beaten*. He desires to win for the sake of winning and honestly believes that he can get anything accomplished. He knows when something is possible and wants to be the doer, the winner, the manager who achieves it.

This is the habit you must cultivate with persistent purpose and will if you are preparing yourself for promotion and leadership in business. A plethora of managers have ambition, many also have the habits of confidence, loyalty, passion, optimism, consistency, and get-up-and-go. Some fewer managers are genuinely determined and persevere despite discouragement. They have an enormous advantage over the others because invincible determination keeps these other habits at work and focusses them on the task in hand. Invincible determination sees the job through until complete. "Derrick, unsuccessful managers in the business world today," said a colleague, "have a lack of application, preparation, and meticulousness. They have ambition but are not willing to struggle to achieve the result."

Willpower and habit are the two most effective instruments for developing persistence. If you desire invincible determination, stand by your purpose and by the best knowledge you can get on the subject. Then, consistently move forward according to that purpose and knowledge.

To follow a purpose when knowledge and reason show that the thing is pointless is mere stubbornness. The insightful sales manager watches closely every indication in the returns from a new sales campaign. If he finds evidence that the campaign is incorrect in organization or method, he changes it. To say, "We planned it that way, and we won't change our minds now," would be foolishness and a waste of time. Invincible determination is not stubbornness. It must be based on knowledge, sound reasoning, and confidence and cannot become an effective habit of character unless it is so based.

However, purpose and knowledge are possible in every situation. No matter how experimental the task, you have some facts to go on, some past experiences to utilize. Call into action observation, concentration, memory, imagination, and your reasoning power. Find the facts founded on judgment and purpose and then proceed.

Proceed unwaveringly and consistently. There *will* be discouragements. Perhaps the office manager who is staying overtime to complete her work knows that her assistant slipped away promptly at the end of the workday with a stack of unfinished work crammed into the desk drawer. Comparison with person watching the clock should not discourage or deter her, however. Invincible determination is personal and individual. The clock-watcher will fail in the long run when it is time for promotion or positions of greater responsibilities. Stick to your task and stay with your purpose. Keep your attention focused on your work because the new awareness which it develops will help you to continue holding on.

Invincible determination involves more than the negative attitude of *don't give up*. Invincible determination is positive and means striving toward a goal with an attitude of going forward to achieve it. It is easy to make this attitude habitual when the goal is certain and not too far in the future.

Set phases to be completed by a given day or hour and then do them. Indecision is a bad habit. The commitment of purpose is a good habit that can be significantly strengthened by the dedication of action-persistence.

Of course, the immeasurable and powerful result of the exercise of will is the adhesive of habit. If you force yourself to keep at this task until you have finished it, you find unshakable determination stronger for the next task. As you tackle this next task, you exercise willpower again; you require yourself to stay until the achievement is accomplished and find determination more natural, more of a habit than ever before. Therefore, it wears its indentation of habit deeper and deeper into your character until it becomes second nature.

Make it second nature to complete every task that you undertake. Keep your get-up-and-go; keep your purpose devoted; and keep your attention focused until you reach the intended goal. Results are what count in business, and invincible determination is the unfailing secret of getting those results.

You may have focused your ambition on a specific goal in business. Continue in it if you have considered carefully and chosen well because there should be no reason for change. You need to move forward to your goal. You need invincible determination, not only as an important principle activating your ambition but also as a working principle applied to the details of your everyday life. You need it in routine business affairs, in the home, in your recreation, and almost everywhere because it needs to be a ruling habit in your life—with no exception.

Apply your willpower to the task or project, to the problem that confronts you, to the book you are reading, to the game you are playing, to the course you are enrolled in, and require yourself to continue until you finish. Continue to be determined. See it all the way through. It will be easier next time.

HABIT 9

Show Initiative

Action is the motto of today's businesses. "Take action," says the chief executive officer to the sales manager. "Bring in the orders," says the sales manager to the sales representatives. "Speed up" is the communication throughout the organization.

Everywhere in business, a manager of action is wanted. The thinker who is not a doer never goes far in his career. However, the thinker who acts, works, and sweats to make his dreams come true moves forward and puts his plan into operation, becoming a manager of initiative. No effort can be applied unless a beginning is made. No progress is made without movement, and no movement can happen without a start. Initiative is a manager's starting power. All beneficial action depends on the ability to make a start, the ability to take the first step, the ability to initiate.

Ambition, get-up-and-go, and invincible determination all pivot on initiative. Your ambition can never be made more than a solemn hope or a lofty wish unless you start to realize it. Get-up-and-go is labor power, and no work is accomplished unless a start is made. You cannot continue in anything that has not begun.

Initiative implies thinking power, not working unconsciously or following the example of someone else, which requires only the ability to emulate. The unconscious manager needs someone to direct him. However, initiative can get him out of this dead-end situation, making him less mechanical, more authentic, and more valuable. The manager of initiative finds new and innovative ways of completing tasks and projects. His mind is alert to every opportunity for time management, trimming expense, or efficiency. He sees the broader view, knows the mission, and understands the reasons behind the reasons. Because of sound judgment, he acts.

Get-up-and-go minus initiative holds the manager at the same level as the average manager. Get-up-and-go without initiative complains about having to perform menial tasks, being passed over for promotion, missing work-life balance, or not having a seat on the board. The moment the manager develops initiative, he becomes too valuable for those issues previously mentioned.

Initiative is a habit that successful managers are made of; and in every business, the manager of initiative is inevitably promoted to greater duties and responsibilities. He moves ahead of the pack, repetitively stepping from a lower position to a higher one as his powers of thought and action strengthen with each use. The manager who needs to be told what to do, when to do it, and how to do it gets a mediocre salary because it is very time-consuming and costly to upper echelon to instruct him. The manager of initiative is invaluable not only because he renders more service but also because he is less expensive to the organization.

The lazy manager has a serious limitation to overcome and will find initiative a weak habit in his character. The difficulty lies in the fact that habits of procrastination and laziness have already become fixed in him. The unwanted effects of a bad start can, however, be overcome with the persistent application of willpower, which will destroy bad habits and substitute right habits of action.

Various mental abilities comprise initiative, along with other character habits. The most important are the powers of observation, imagination, and reasoning and the habits of confidence, get-up-and-go, and ambition.

As a manager of initiative, I have learned to be alert; my senses must be accurate and active. I must be quick to notice significant details that call for action. My imagination must be able to perceive possibilities and construct actionable plans. I must have clear judgment, or I will act on doubtful foundations and rush to ill-considered conclusions. To give strength and character to my initiative, I am motivated by my organization's mission. This enables me to have confidence and get-up-and-go. If you develop these intellectual influences and these character habits, you will provide a significant basis for initiative. It is unlikely that a manager who has cultivated these qualities to a normal degree will lack initiative.

Willpower is needed because it is the key factor in the development of other habits, and it is of greatest importance. Some managers suppress creative action simply because they are in the routine of deferring to someone else. Fear of failure also prevents countless managers from taking the initiative. Such fear erodes individuality and robs the manager of original thought.

The manager becomes mechanical because it is easy to follow but difficult to lead. Many are followers but very few are leaders. It only requires observation and memory to follow; however, it requires imagination, judgment, and courage to lead and initiate things.

Assert yourself whenever the urge arises to suppress a new idea that you think is worth trying. The fast-paced business world of today is concerned with looking for new and innovative ideas. You may have a normal tendency to stay in the background; therefore, asserting yourself may be a new experience. It is, however, a necessary experience if you are to become a successful manager. Force yourself to respond to that which you know is important. Commit yourself to the idea of action so that initiative can be unleashed.

As you respond to your desire to act, you will find your control of action growing. You will find it easier to allow free will initiative next time, and as initiative becomes a habit of action, you will grow strong in all your business knowledge, skills, and abilities. You will think constructively and act decisively.

You will find your character growing in confidence, in ambition, in get-up-and-go. You will find yourself repeatedly realizing the attribute of leadership, and as the habits of a successful manager develop in you, you will notice increasing opportunities for you to use them.

The manager of initiative keeps his chest up, back straight, and head erect; he inspires confidence and respect. He respects himself, and others respect him. He is not conceited. The manager who is always advertising to the world how much he knows is the manager who knows very little. The manager who truly knows also realizes that the knowledge, skills, and abilities he possesses are but a tiny part of the whole. It is the teachable mind that learns. The arrogantly confident manager, who prides himself on never changing his opinion, has reached the limit of his development.

Keep an unbiased mind and let life be your teacher. Learn sometimes by the other managers' mistakes. Do not be the one who must always put her hand into the fire to be convinced that it burns. Also, you may learn from another manager's success. A manager is not only known by the company she keeps, but she becomes like the company she keeps. The least member of a group of intellectuals is going to learn more than the highest manager in an unproductive group. Do not view yourself as a part of a large, struggling mass, out of which so few managers are destined to climb that it is futile to try. Instead, think of yourself as already a successful manager and your work as a stepping-stone to higher duties and responsibilities.

Notice the difference between the manager who goes to the office in the morning with the feeling that there's another day to drag through, another pile of work to plow over, and the manager of initiative who feels that this is his opportunity to prove his value, to take a step toward upward mobility. The first manager's eyes are dull, his step lagging, his entire demeanor a weary protest to the monotony of life. The second manager does not know that life is monotonous. He never has time to find it out. To him, each new day is an opportunity for achievement, perhaps the guardian of the moment that will mark another milestone in his career.

When the manager of initiative enters his office in the morning, even the customer service representative feels it. Coming in with a full, swinging stride, his entire body alert and poised, his eyes shining with confidence and ambition, he radiates magnetic get-up-and-go and invincible determination that becomes a fountain of inspiration to all who are associated with him. His directors have confidence in him because they respect that he knows what he is passionate about, and they trust he cannot make the best of himself without also doing the best thing for the organization. He is the manager they will promote when the position becomes available. He is the manager they will absorb into the organization rather than have him depart to become a competitor.

This manager of initiative will never tell you he lost his position because the executives were jealous of him. He knows executives want proficiency and that they keep and promote the manager who gives them what they want. He knows business character matters. His mind is his own, and he takes care that it is competent. He sees to it that his brain, his most valuable instrument, is made more effective by reading books and journals. He pursues conversation with managers of deep intellectual minds. He learns to concentrate and does not allow his mind to wander. He is its master, and it thinks as he directs it. He masters his destiny because he has mastered himself.

HABIT 10

Master Self-Control

Jiu-Jitsu is the Japanese art of self-defense. Founded on meticulous science, jiu-jitsu was developed by generation after generation of men who devoted their lives to its perfecting. A master in jiu-jitsu is a formidable opponent. By the carefully placed pressure of a finger, he can cause his enemy to collapse, squirming in pain. No physical or muscular strength can stand against his accurate knowledge of the weak spots of his opponent, coupled with knowledge of his powers and how to use them. The master of jiu-jitsu is first a master of self-control.

To become an apprentice of jiu-jitsu, one must be recognized as worthy. Then he is required to give several years of his life to the mastery of himself. He must put himself through a long course of training until he has developed complete control of his body and mind. This means that he only eats the simplest food and in the smallest quantity necessary for good health; he does not drink intoxicants; he controls his temper and emotions. When the apprentice has become the commander of his body, mind, and character, he is trained in the fighting art of jiu-jitsu. Determinedly, patiently, and optimistically, through ten years, he studies, practices, and perfects himself, until he becomes a master—afraid of no one. Unarmed, he can defend himself against half a dozen men with swords. He knows his power and is in control of all his abilities, which makes him the master over hostility.

Managers can learn this lesson of self-control, self-command, and self-mastery. All the training and education received through life and career provides the ability to do so, yet few will reach such a milestone. The nearer a manager approaches the idea of self-control, the more he realizes in himself the idea of the exceptional character because self-control, accurately working, will inspire and calm all the character habits. Self-Control is the engagement of willpower, and a strong will is the largest factor in fixing good habits of feeling and action.

The most successful managers are those who are self-controlled; they are managers of influence. They have mastered their feelings and capabilities, which results in their ability to effectively lead, mentor, and guide others.

Self-control means not only the mastery of body and mind but also a mastery of the feelings. Working through knowledge, skills, and abilities alone will not provide the best return on investment—especially if a manager is insensitive, impolite, bad-tempered, irritable, overbearing, thoughtless, insulting, disloyal, and often angry. All of these traits are signs of weakness. The strong manager is self-controlled.

When a manager loses control of himself, no one else is responsible. The results are always hurtful, if not disastrous, both to himself and to others. I have witnessed this firsthand. The customary excuses, "I can't help it," or "I'm built that way," or "It's my nature" do not excuse such loss of self-control. The arrogant manager who says, "I don't let anyone run over me," or "Nobody can push me around," or "Get out of my way or get ran over" displays the worst type of false pride: the blind and unthinking kind.

Certainly, situations arise in which we lose our temper, go into a rage, and hit back. But just what is meant when you say, "I can't help it?" Isn't that a direct confession of weakness? Isn't it an admission of failure within yourself to control emotions? You are confessing that circumstances are stronger than your personality. When you say, "I'm built that way; it's my nature," you condemn your artistry because you had a hand in becoming who you are. You are your builder, your nature is you, and you are exactly what you have been thinking, feeling, and doing.

Therefore, if you desire to make your character strong, you must take your old nature and build it into a new one. You do not have to keep the old nature just because you have it. You can change it with willpower, by bringing habits under control. Moreover, the most important reason for self-control is that it makes an excellent manager out of you, a strong manager who will not yield to every hostile situation that may cross its path.

Self-respect should provoke a manager to self-control. No one who has high regard for himself will permit himself to be impolite—it is unprofessional. Self-respect lifts us above the insignificant aggravations and irritations that frequently cause managers to lose self-control.

The self-controlled manager knows that self-control means self-preservation. Certainly, you desire a long life, happiness, and enough money for your needs. Controlling and directing your influences and emotions will lead these benefits to you. Ambition is achieved as you control your time, determination, and desires for comfort and pleasure. This may be difficult, but it is for self-preservation that you eat in moderation, reduce alcohol consumption, and exercise weekly. Self-control is the watchdog that enables you to carry out the drive of ambition.

My grandmother taught me two laws of life: the Law of Effort and Response and the Law of Personal Responsibility. Once I maturely understood them, I was able to bring all my influences and emotions under control. It takes a steady force of habit, but it is achievable.

The Law of Effort and Response means that you receive back to yourself the same kind of thoughts and actions you send into the world. It is the age-old principle of sowing and reaping. If you are complaining and irritable, your associates will tend to be irritated, complaining, and insensitive. If you are cheerful, kind, and thoughtful under all circumstances, you will be met by the same behaviors in others. Test this law through actual practice. Do not be concerned with the other person's behavior or habits. Rather, focus on being courteous, thoughtful, optimistic, hopeful, luminous, sociable, and polite in your treatment of him. Watch for change in his attitude. It is inevitable.

The Law of Personal Responsibility says you hold the responsibility for what you become in health, intelligence, character, and behavior. You cannot get away from that responsibility. The only practical thing to do is to acquire mastery over all your influences and emotions—to control them. You can do this through the power of choice. What you choose to do, you can do up to the limit of your capacity.

The self-controlled manager is confident in himself. Self-control shows itself in masterful poise, in strength to control impulses and emotions under all situations. His get-up-and-go and intelligence will carry him to almost any desired height. He knows that no matter how many difficulties may face him, no matter how many people may be against him, no matter what may happen to set him back, he will pull through. His will governs his feelings, and good judgment directs his acts. His mind functions clearly and calmly.

However, self-control is not the usual honor of every manager. How may it be developed? How can a manager gain mastery of his influences and emotions? How can he direct his abilities so that he remains calm, poised, smiling, happy, and composed under any aggravation?

Willpower—a trained and intelligent will working under perfect discipline—is the best helper to self-control. If you direct your willpower to develop the other habits of character, you will find it already trained and capable of assisting you with self-control.

In developing self-control, you will find it necessary to use your willpower in various ways: (1) to deny or prevent an undesirable thought or act; (2) to force yourself to take time before accepting a decision; (3) to require yourself to do the thing your judgment dictates is the right thing, even if it is difficult.

First, quit excusing yourself for your weakness. Give up the habit of blaming the other person. This is essential because as long as you excuse your mistakes or faults, you will make no effort to overcome them. If you blame others and avoid your responsibility, you develop in yourself a habit of circumventing and sidestepping—behavior that is destructive not only for self-control but also for confidence and honesty. Self-mastery begins with an honest acknowledgment of one's faults and a severe disapproval of them.

Second, think before you decide or act. Whenever the temptation is to respond to a provoking remark, to bite back, to dodge duty, to evade responsibility, or to act on impulse rather than on reason, stop and think. Remember the Law of Effort and Response and put it into practice. Remember the Law of Personal Responsibility; you are accountable for what you do or say. Be certain that you say and do the right thing. Keep the upper hand and make your will—not your feelings, impulses, or the outside influences of the environment—the dominant, controlling factor.

Third, compel yourself to do what your reason tells you is the right thing to do. Often your impulse will prompt you to some other action;

you will not want to do the right thing; a stubborn tendency will clash with your reason and sense of right. Nevertheless, willpower can lead if you exercise it. Self-discipline is possible to have and engage in every situation, both in the minor routine and the big emergency.

Self-control involves obedience—willing obedience. You must make yourself obey your reason and your will, not because of fear but because reason and will are master. Be the master of your speech and guard your tongue so that it will not speak until you are ready. Impulses have their place, but they are beyond the will. Even when your impulses are worthy, to allow them to dictate is to undermine self-control.

Avoid urge and emotional action. Weigh motives and apply judgment and reason. Live up to your ideals and do not give way to feelings, impulses, and emotions. The strong manager controls his actions, even under passionate incitement, because he is the master of himself.

With such rules of conduct, you will develop habits of self-control. Do not permit excuses, no matter how believable they may seem, and do not dodge responsibility, no matter how severe the consequences. By forcing yourself to think and deliberate before taking action, you develop habits of consistency as well as self-control. By obeying your reason and sense of what is right, by disciplining yourself regardless of the immediate consequences, you establish reason and fairness as guiding principles in your life and career, providing the ideal environment for self-control to flourish.

Rule yourself and you rule your creating power, your earning power, and your achieving power. You control your destiny and build your future in any organization.

CHAPTER THREE

Use It or Lose It

What is it that makes the difference between efficiency and inefficiency? Why is it that some managers are broad-minded, big-hearted, and sympathetic, while others are trivial, narrow-minded, and mean in their purposes and actions? Why is it that some managers repeatedly receive greater duties and responsibilities with promotion, while others drift along on a mundane level of everyday existence?

The difference is essentially one of development: what traits have been cultivated in the manager's life? The meticulously resourceful manager is the one who is the most successful. This means the manager is healthy, mentally keen, and capable; he has developed The Ten Habits of Highly Successful Managers.

For example, ambition is an important character habit, but unless it is secured by persistence and self-control, it may become a wild, ineffective, and even destructive quality. Loyalty without consistency may degenerate into excessive tenderness. Initiative without invincible determination goes nowhere, accomplishing nothing more than a sequence of starts and modifications. Passion without confidence and get-up-and-go is just talk.

The habits must work together, and they do work together for maximum results. When ambition is backed by confidence and consistency—made capable by get-up-and-go, initiative, and invincible determination; inspired by passion and optimism; secured by loyalty; and regulated by self-control—it overcomes roadblocks, overrides obstacles, and accomplishes worthwhile results. It is when the ten habits are in active cooperation that each is strongest and most effective.

The one-habit manager may keep his position, or he may even be promoted to higher positions. For example, consistency is such a desirable habit that many grumpy managers are retained and eventually promoted simply because they can be depended on. But optimism and passion in his work would surely make him more valuable, appreciated, and desirable. Both traits would increase his attention and his effectiveness in the teamwork of the organization.

Therefore, each separate habit is much more valuable and efficient because of the reinforcement of other habits. No manager should be satisfied with anything less than an exceptionally developed character because the well-rounded character is the only satisfactory character in business. In character development, specialization may not bring the best results. In every branch of business and every position, the ten habits are needed: the assistant manager as well as the general manager; the production manager as well as the superintendent; and the bank manager as well as the bank president. Each will be a better manager or executive in business, with a brighter outlook of success, if he is not only energetic and ambitious but also confident, loyal, and consistent. He must be strengthened by habits of initiative, invincible determination, and self-control. Optimism and passion can elevate him to the highest standard.

The difference in development between habits is a difference in quality. If your consistency is stronger than your passion, you have simply developed stronger habits of consistency than of passion. Sometimes a habit seems to be absent because some managers do not have passion, ambition, or confidence. But in every case, the basic habit is there, even though it may be no more than a long-neglected tendency, an inclination, or a hope. Persistent exercise will develop the tendency into a fixed habit and produce character of higher quality.

Developed ambition or developed confidence is of a higher quality than the undeveloped habit, just as refined gold is of a higher quality than the raw mineral. Likewise, every manager is gifted with these critical characteristics to some degree, but their ultimate quality and usefulness

BUSINESS CHARACTER MATTERS

depend on the degree of their development. Your decisions determine whether they are trained and exercised into strength and efficiency or whether they weaken and degenerate.

If they weaken and degenerate, it is because you did not use them. For example, confidence may be undermined by doubts and fears that overcome the confident impulse, denying it expression and hindering its exercise. Through non-use, the habit becomes weakened. Habits of timidity and doubt take the place of habits of confidence, and the original habit becomes a tiny drop in the ocean of character.

Just as your lungs are made stronger through breathing exercises, your character habits grow as they are used. In fact, they will only grow if they are used. It is through use that we get benefit from any possession. Only by using technology, using money, using machinery, using materials, using brains, using muscles, or using human abilities are we able to make these possessions return profits or satisfaction of any kind.

While most material possessions wear out or are spent in use, human abilities grow stronger and more powerful as they are called into operation. In using money, you spend it; it is gone. In using technology and machinery, you wear out its parts. Every day it is used, the machine depreciates.

In contrast, in using a muscle, you not only get the advantage of its present service but you also strengthen it for future service. In using your powers of observation, concentration, memory, imagination, and the other mental abilities, you get benefit now, and are, at the same time, making these powers more efficient for the next demand placed upon them. In exercising ambition, loyalty, consistency, and other character habits, you are getting the double advantage of present achievement and preparedness for future achievement as a successful manager.

Another striking difference should be noted between material possessions and human abilities. If you stop using money and store it away, you can obtain it for full value at any time. If you store technology or a machine, you not only save it from normal wear and tear, but it will also be at your service when you need it. However, keep any human ability in inactivity, and you will destroy it. Unused muscles, mental powers, and character habits will weaken and degenerate through non-use.

Human abilities are largely dependent upon habit. Habit dominates our thinking, feeling, and doing. Whether we will see it or not, we fall into habits—generally, bad habits. The manager who does not force himself to develop habits of get-up-and-go and invincible determination will inevitably fall into habits of lethargy. Unless habits of consistency are developed, the careless habits of the clock-watcher or the dodger will grow up like weeds. You will have habits, and unless you see to it that they are good, healthy, and useful, they will be bad habits that hold you back from progress rather than propelling you into the active teamwork of the modern business world.

What will your character be? Will it matter in your organization? It is up to you to choose whether it will be strengthened and made more effective or whether it will be left to hit-or-miss development. If you are truly ambitious for success, you must choose the policy of positive, constructive development. You now know that only managers of character can achieve the positions of leadership in an organization. Working only with your hands and brain will satisfy in repetitive service, but places of responsibility demand the manager of character who can be depended upon. Business character matters. With your willpower in control, you can change any habit into a habit that will serve you in every aspect of your career and life. Concentrate, practice, and use them.

CHAPTER FOUR

Diversity and Inclusion

When successful managers draw on the wisdom of a workforce that reflects the population we serve, we are better able to understand and meet the needs of our customers: the American people. Across the United States, managers have made commendable progress toward hiring a workforce that truly reflects America's diversity, and we must continue to pursue that goal. But merely hiring a diverse workforce is not enough. We must ensure our workplaces become more inclusive as well.

America was founded on the idea that from many, we are one, a whole that is greater than the sum of its parts. That is the rationale for inclusion. To gain the maximum benefit from our increasingly diverse workforce, we must make every employee feel welcome and motivated to work her hardest and rise through the ranks. We must affirm that we work better together because of our differences, not despite them.

When we tap into this knowledge, when employees are trained in team building, decision-making, problem-solving, and conflict resolution, we will not only uphold the principles of our nation, but we will also get better results.

The business case for inclusion is clear in American history. The best, brightest, and hardest workers have come to America for over two centuries because they knew they would have an opportunity to join our society, work hard, and succeed.

Workforce diversity is defined by the United States Office of Personnel Management, Office of Diversion and Inclusion as a collection of individual attributes that together help the organization pursue its objectives efficiently and effectively.

Inclusion is defined as a set of behaviors (culture) that encourages employees to feel valued for their unique qualities and experience a sense of belonging.

Inclusive diversity is defined as a set of behaviors that promote collaboration amongst a diverse group.

A diverse workforce in an inclusive environment will improve individual and organizational performance and result in better value to customers, clients, taxpayers, and other stakeholders.

Diversity and inclusion provide organizations a path for creating and fostering a workforce that includes and engages employees drawn from all segments of society. Managers should increase the transparency of human capital processes (to the extent appropriate) throughout the organizational workplace to foster inclusion that leads to diversity in the workforce. Organizations must fully utilize policies, programs, and systems that support inclusive diversity through increasingly focused, innovative, and accelerated communication and learning strategies.

Managers may work with their Human Resources colleagues as they focus on data-driven decision-making through the strategic use of applicant flow data from past selection processes. This will help to plan recruitment for subsequent selection processes so as to foster a diversified applicant pool at all stages of the employee life-cycle, emphasize and identify potential areas of implicit bias, understand the New Inclusion Quotient (New IQ), create a more interactive Equal Opportunity Recruitment Program (EORP), and intensify and accelerate organization communication techniques.

The federal government had multiple roundtable sessions and extensive consultation with inclusive diversity experts and academics. The following insights were shared:

    a.   More tools and training are needed to analyze applicant flow data thoroughly.

b. The employee lifecycle is full of potential adverse impacts resulting from implicit biases.

c. Social media is under-utilized for recruitment/outreach.

d. A general lack of urgency to create inclusively diverse organizations permeates the system.

e. No widely accepted method to measure or identify inclusion or inclusive behaviors is used.

f. More Inclusive Diversity (ID) professionals, who are well-versed, knowledgeable, and skilled in change management, are needed.

g. A robust and consistent way to measure Equal Opportunity (EO) progress outside of roundtables and representation tracking is needed.

Organizations must foster the diversity of the potential applicant pool throughout all stages of the employee lifecycle. This can be accomplished through targeted and strategic outreach and recruitment efforts from the Human Resources manager, including the use of social media as part of an overall and comprehensive recruitment plan. Awareness must be raised about the potential impact cognitive biases can have on all stages of the employee lifecycle process. These "decision or selection" stages can have a significant impact on the upward mobility and level of engagement employees may experience within the workplace, and it is important to support a system where the impact of any such biases is minimized.

To foster workforce engagement, emphasize inclusion that causes members to feel valued and to experience a sense of belonging. Aim for improving (or at least sustaining, if already close to optimal) Inclusion Index scores using the New IQ approach and process. If most organizations use Employee Resource Groups (ERGs), which are grassroots groups formed by employees across all demographics—race, national origin, gender, sexual orientation, disability, education, geography, military status, occupation, etc. and Special Emphasis Program Managers (SEPMs), who ensure that agencies take affirmative steps to provide equal opportunity to minorities, women and people with disabilities in all areas of employment. Both provide the potential for a "critical mass" of employees to increase workplace inclusion.

The increased demand for innovation and efficiency may present challenges in projecting and meeting future human resources needs. Organizations can address these challenges with a diverse and inclusive workforce built by casting a broad net in the search for top talent, wherever it may be found. Organizations that, consistent with merit system principles, employ a workforce that draws from all corners of America—in filling positions from entry level to the executive level—will create a culture that fosters creativity and benefits from a greater return on investments in the workforce. In short, a commitment to equal opportunity, diversity, and inclusion is critical to accomplishing your organization's mission.

Creating a diverse workforce that draws from all segments of society requires a sustained commitment to ensuring a level playing field upon which applicants and employees may compete for opportunities within your organization. Sustaining the highest levels of integrity and professionalism throughout new outreach and recruiting efforts is paramount to achieving the organization's vision.

An organization seeking diversity should follow these three goals:

1. Diversify the workforce through active engagement of leadership: Organizations must foster a diverse, high-performing workforce drawn from all segments of American society.
2. Include and engage everyone in the workplace: Organizations must foster a culture that encourages employees to feel uniquely valued and experience a sense of belonging.
3. Optimize inclusive diversity efforts using data-driven approaches: Organizations must continue to improve their inclusive diversity communication efforts and comply in a timely fashion with EORP requirements, if established.

Goal 1: Diversify the Workforce through Active Engagement of Leadership

Organizational leaders must continue their efforts to attract, retain, and cultivate diverse managers by frequently communicating, accounting for, and modeling inclusive diversity behaviors that attract and reflect the broad diversity of American society.

Rationale

Managers are the leaders critical to inclusive diversity efforts because they can direct the necessary attention and resources (intensity) toward inclusive diversity programs and policies. Managers can promote progress by communicating the importance of inclusive diversity by speaking, modeling, and accounting for it.

A diverse workforce has been positively associated with greater talent utilization, better employee retention, increased innovation, and higher performance. To achieve this, managers must emphasize the importance of inclusive diversity by integrating this value within all forms of organizational communications, including social media channels, company websites, and interoffice correspondence. Effective communications should be cascaded from senior leadership down to first-line supervision.

To improve inclusive diversity efforts, managers should consider each major diversity effort through an assortment of possible innovation strategies. One promising strategy utilized by many successful organizations is Human-Centered Design, a problem-solving process that the US Office of Personnel Management (OPM) has championed. The Human-Centered Design (HCD) process can be applied to each inclusive diversity strategy, process, or program to generate original ideas and effectively achieve positive results.

Priority 1.1: Managers emphasize the importance of their inclusive diversity efforts by utilizing a wide range of communication strategies and tools that demonstrate their support for these initiatives. Specifically, managers must provide resources and support to identify and overcome the cognitive, motivational, and structural barriers that inhibit inclusive diversity efforts.

Priority 1.2: Managers review the wide range of policies, programs, systems, and techniques currently in use and determine specific initiatives that should be enhanced and improved. The evaluation should include diversity, inclusion, and engagement elements in performance plans; employee resource groups; mentoring and coaching; and inclusive diversity training.

Priority 1.3: Managers develop and implement broad outreach strategies to attract leaders from diverse sources to the organization, consistent with merit system principles, through strategic partnerships with affinity organizations, diverse postsecondary educational institutions, professional associations, and public, private, and non-profit sectors.

Goal 2: Include and Engage Everyone in the Workplace

Organizations must intensify efforts to foster cultures that encourage employees to feel valued for their unique qualities and experience a sense of belonging, engagement, and connection to the mission of the agency.

Rationale

Of concern is the continued underrepresentation of people who identify themselves as Hispanic. Another challenge is recruiting qualified individuals across multiple cultures into the workforce to prepare for anticipated retirements, the continued difficulty in recruiting minorities and women to fill Science, Technology, Engineering, and Mathematics (STEM) designated positions, and the continued difficulty in recruiting minorities and women to fill executive-level positions. One critical driver of employee engagement is a strong, inclusive culture founded upon the emphasis of inclusive behaviors.

To help agencies create an inclusive culture, OPM has developed a new strategy called the New Inclusion Quotient or New IQ, which is an initiative designed to help employees and managers foster diversity and inclusion in the workplace. The New IQ, successfully applied, will enable agencies to engage better and more fully utilize the inherent talent of their respective workforce. If organizations did the same, the results might be phenomenal.

Priority 2.1: Foster a culture of inclusion and engagement by employing culture change strategies. Provide training and education on cultural competency, implicit bias awareness, and inclusion learning for all employees.

Priority 2.2: Assess, redesign, and re-engineer organizational structures and business processes to promote teamwork, collaboration, cross-functional operations, and transparency. Likewise, deconstruct organizational systems that lead to exclusive cultures and flawed decision-making.

Goal 3: Optimize Inclusive Diversity Efforts Using Data-Driven Approaches

Organizations must intensify efforts to create and foster diverse, high-performing workforces. This effort is aided by utilizing data-driven approaches and optimizing policies, processes, and programs to drive inclusive diversity efforts.

Rationale

It is critical that organizations apply a more sophisticated inclusive diversity approach by using the latest data-driven techniques. By applying data-driven techniques, organizations can better identify hard to recognize problems that limit diversity in their respective departments. This more evidence-based approach could reduce the negative impact of implicit biases and promote better decision-making and talent utilization.

To optimize policy design and practices, organizations need to develop a cohesive structure to identify and manage the impact of any implicit biases throughout all levels of the employee lifecycle. This increased focus on addressing implicit bias will enrich the data organizations use to support inclusive diversity policy development and operations.

Priority 3.1: Create a diverse, high-performing workforce by utilizing data-driven approaches to recruitment. This must include analyzing applicant flow data; educating hiring managers; and designing fair and effective recruitment and examining strategies that cast the broadest net possible and apply merit principles. Also consider utilizing applicable special hiring authorities as supplements to competitive hiring processes; partnering with diverse organizations and institutions to recruit from all segments of society; and conducting a review of potential implicit biases within the organization.

Priority 3.2: Promote a diverse, high-performing workforce by utilizing data-driven approaches to promotion opportunities and career development. This must include analyzing applicant flow data; developing career enhancement opportunities; utilizing appropriate collaborative practices and social media technologies; and collaborating with program managers, affinity groups, and employee resource groups.

Priority 3.3: Collect relevant performance data to establish a business case for diversity and inclusion for the agency; collaborate with other organizations and the diversity and inclusion subject matter experts to create models for analyzing performance metrics in correlation with diversity and inclusion metrics.

President Obama's Executive Order 13583 states, "Our Nation derives strength from the diversity of its population and its commitment to equal opportunity for all. We are at our best when we draw on the talents of all parts of our society, and our greatest accomplishments are achieved when diverse perspectives are brought to bear to overcome our greatest challenges."

Managers, once you have achieved a diverse workforce in an inclusive environment, it will improve individual and organizational performance.

CHAPTER FIVE

The Successful Manager

L eadership requires the successful manager to possess certain personality qualities and methods of dealing with his team. The first consideration is to understand the object of leadership. Getting a clear idea of the object of a task should always be the first step. Teams work better and managers lead better when the object of their efforts is clearly defined.

Everything you do and think is a product of the simplest beginnings. The most profound thinker who ever lived first had to learn the alphabet. Step by step, we learn and grow. Just remember that Abraham Lincoln and Ulysses S. Grant, in their small towns, must often have become discouraged and thought that the future seemed hopeless. However, systematically, these two men found their way to fame and glory, each becoming president of the United States of America—the greatest democracy in the world.

If you knowingly walk toward your goal to become a successful manager, one self-aware step is like ten in the dark. Do not be troubled at being passed by unsuccessful managers. The distance covered at the end, the friendships you will make, and the good you will accomplish—the total record—is what counts.

The successful manager knows business character matters. Character is the honorable possession of a successful manager, and it dignifies every exalted position held in an organization. Character exercises a greater power than wealth and secures all the honor without the jealousies of fame. It carries with it an influence, which always delivers. It is the result of proven integrity, politeness, and consistency—qualities which command the overall confidence and respect of an entire organization.

Successful managers with great business character are not only the integrity of their departments but also the best motivational influence on the entire organization. The core strength of businesses depends on individual character, and the very foundations of their brand rest on it.

The possession of good character is one of the highest objects of life. Having a high standard of life, even though we may not be able overall to realize it, is crucial. Integrity in word and deed is the backbone of character and loyal adherence to genuineness its most prominent characteristic.

Truthfulness in action, as well as in words, is essential to the respectability of character. A manager must be what he seems or purports to be. If he respects himself and values the respect of others, he will honestly do what he intends to do, priding himself on his integrity and meticulousness. Managers whose acts are at direct variance with their words command no respect, and what they say has little weight. Even when truth is expressed, it seems annoying from their lips.

True character does the right thing, even when no one is watching and is strengthened and supported by the development of good habits. Managers I consulted with all remarked on the strength of habit and insisted its power comes from repetition in act and thought. I could not agree more.

You have learned The Top Ten Habits of Highly Successful Managers, those that propel managers forward in business and win for them places of greater responsibility and leadership as executives. The fundamentals of business character are the total of these ten strong and active habits. It is not enough, for example, to be ambitious. The ambitious manager who lacks confidence, loyalty, passion, optimism, consistency, get-up-and-go, invincible determination, initiative, and self-control cannot become successful.

Wherever formed, habit acts involuntarily and without effort. It is only when you oppose it that you find how powerful habit has become.

At first, the habit may seem to have no more strength than a spider's web; however, once formed, it becomes a strong, binding force. The small events of life, taken singly, may seem remarkably unimportant, like snow that falls silently, but, flake by flake, by accumulation, these snowflakes can form an avalanche.

As habit strengthens with age and character becomes formed, turning in a new direction becomes more and more difficult. It is often harder to unlearn what has been learned. To replace an old habit is sometimes a more painful and difficult thing than to pull a tooth. Habits infiltrate all parts of life. Thus, it has been said, "The wisest habit of all is the habit of care in the formation of good habits."

The following are good habits over sixty-five successful managers have noted as beneficial to the business leader:

Morals and Manners

Morals and manners, which give color to life, are neither more nor less than good behavior. Comprised of courtesy, kindness, and goodwill, morals and manners are useful in pleasant interaction between human beings. "Civility," said Shakespeare's Lady Montague, "costs nothing and buys everything."

Manners are the adornment of action; speaking a kind word or doing a kind thing greatly enhances the value of our actions. What seems to be done with dislike or as an act of arrogance is hardly accepted as a favor. Some managers pride themselves on their grouchiness; and though they may possess value and productiveness, their manner is often such as to render them intolerable. It is difficult to like a manager who habitually wounds your self-respect and takes pride in saying offensive things to you. Others are extremely patronizing and cannot avoid seizing on every small opportunity of making their greatness felt.

The successful manager is one whose character has been shaped after the highest models. He values his character. As he respects himself, he respects others and prioritizes manners and civility in all his interactions.

Getting along with People

If you respect people, try to connect with them, rather than hiding behind your desk. Study your team with sensitivity and try to contribute something to their success and happiness. Be reasonably generous with your thoughts and time, and though you have a partial reserve with everyone, portray an outward reserve with no one. In doing so, you will get along with your executives, supervisors, colleagues, and team. Managers wise enough to make human relations the main concern will prosper.

The successful manager guards his self-respect and that of his team. Self-respect is essential to self-confidence, and self-confidence is essential for each man to play his part successfully. If work is to progress efficiently, the leader will be constantly called upon to make decisions and to act upon them. Each must, therefore, have enough self-confidence to do this without running to someone to ask what to do. Those of high character do not "pass the buck" of responsibility.

Self-Respect within the Manager

The manager must maintain his self-respect—with life, people, and in the performance of the position held. His relations with his seniors and direct leaders; his knowledge of his job; his self-control of temper, triviality, pettiness, etc.; his methods of directing work and handling staff—all these are to influence and signal his self-respect. He must realize that he stands before his staff as a manager. And in this light, he wants to be an inspiration, not an apology. Superior knowledge, abilities, and moral qualities determine one's fitness for leadership and solicit the staff's loyalty and respect. It is not the size or age of the body but what emanates from the soul within it that makes the leader.

Self-Respect of the Team

The manager must value the self-respect of his staff, whether a small group or a large team. He needs their intelligent cooperation and must often depend on their judgment and willingness to carry on without specific instructions. Unless the staff believe in themselves and feel that he believes in them, they will lack the confidence to decide what to do and be afraid to do it, for fear of failure and its consequences.

So, by showing confidence in them, by never ignoring them as individuals, by encouraging and commending good work, as well as correcting the error, the manager develops the self-respect of his staff as a sure basis for the self-confidence and strength of character they need to meet his requirements.

Qualifying for Managership

In the Navy, several men and women fitted themselves to lead successfully. Hundreds of thousands of young Americans fitted themselves to lead as commissioned and non-commissioned officers. Many had no previous experience of command to guide them, had never given a direction. But by application, they rapidly learned how to handle themselves successfully as leaders and their personnel as loyal followers. No one expects perfection. Likewise, in business, it is impracticable to follow the rules or to assume qualities that are not natural. The thing to do is to realize that leadership may be developed, that you may absorb its ordinary fundamentals into your system. Then study yourself as you apply the principles of leadership to the problems of your position.

You must understand your personality. Learn to appreciate its strong points and its weak ones, its possibilities for doing the right thing and the wrong, and its probable effect on others. Get it under control through practicing self-control and make it work intelligently for you. You will make mistakes—the best managers do. The point is to have sense enough to recognize the mistake, correct it, and try to avoid repeating it. Assess yourself and observe others, asking in each case if the best thing was done to get the desired result.

Generally, there's one best thing to say or do and at least a dozen wrong ones. The chances are largely in favor of using the wrong approach, but by giving it thought, you learn to pick the right one. In the end, it becomes consistently habitual for you to do so. When you think seriously about yourself in your job and determine that you are going to be authentic, sincere, fair, and self-controlled, you realize that your team is comprised of human beings and that you lead them through *your* personality. Therefore, study your personality and your habits so you may use them intelligently. Observation and personal application of your findings are great things.

No two managers will act exactly alike; each must use his personality. One may be naturally cold, abrupt, and stern, the other polite and gentle, yet both can be equally good leaders. But when you analyze their treatment of their personnel, you will find that both observe the same fundamental principles of impartiality, fairness, and regard for individual development.

As the personalities of managers must differ, those of the personnel may present even greater diversity. To direct them, develop a working knowledge of human nature. In some circumstances, all people respond with similar instinct and habits; at other times, you must consider the individual. Here is where observation, experience, and thinking prepare you to act intelligently. You must instinctively know what touch to give to get the result you want. If you are not sure what to do, think what would make you respond optimistically if you were in her place and what would make you move. Let this decide what you will do. It will generally be the right thing because, at the core, we are all pretty much the same.

Above all, you must be genuine. You must use the personality God gave you. Use it naturally and with an earnest purpose to play the game fairly. If by nature, you are kind and tactful, do not try to be a lion because you have seen and admired some big, growling manager who was a successful leader. The genuineness and sincerity of your efforts will go further than the best possible imitation of some other.

Self-Control

Self-control is the first step toward the ability to direct others. So, observe human nature and note the characteristics of the self-disciplined manager versus the manager who is not. Those managers who allow an undisciplined assistant manager to be promoted to manager put a great burden on the organization and a great hindrance on that manager. Selfish, short-tempered, volatile, and self-centered, he is a poor member of the team and is more often tolerated by his colleagues than enthusiastically welcomed. He has many hard lessons to learn before he appreciates the true value in the career ahead of him or becomes a truly worthwhile member of an organization. Far from being fit to lead others, he is generally the most difficult problem for the executive, who now must do the work that the manager should have done when he was an assistant.

You may assume that you have the necessary business character for managership or you would not be in a position to use it. It is for you to prove your worth by improving in The Ten Habits of Highly Successful Managers. You will not do this by cutting corners or even by faking it until you make it. You can only do it by continued thoughtfulness in meeting the human problems of your position and by disciplining yourself, which will make and keep you prepared for your duties.

Consideration for the Rights of Others

It is a good thing for every manager to realize that he is part of a community whose members are each entitled to the same consideration he would give himself. This certainly is important for the manager who is responsible for the conduct of others. Everyone hates a bully as a candidate for promotion in business or community. You see him elbowing women and older adults aside as he crowds himself to the front at a high-profile event. Throughout a busy day on the job, you'll see him jamming and trampling others to get the best for himself. He gains a questionable satisfaction for his swollen ego but elicits the disdain of his colleagues who have thought enough about business character to realize that his type is an outrage and far from desirable as a characteristic of the organization.

Put Yourself in Her Place

If you want to get someone to do something, mentally put yourself in her place. This is not only a tactful way to win compliance, but it also brings joy to all concerned. In presenting an idea by this method, you give your attention to the form and way you present it, rather than concentrate all your thought on the idea alone. It requires only a bit of consideration to discern the probable feelings and thoughts of the other. Simply ask yourself how you would feel in her place. The manager who has won his promotion from the lowest levels has an advantage in having experienced the point of view of his staff. Too often, however, he throws it away and exhibits a case of the big head by yelling, "Hey you!" in absolute disregard of the outraged feelings which he must know this always provokes.

It is more efficient to be tactful and considerate. To accomplish it, you must sacrifice excessive pride. This will get better results and make work life worth living for everyone.

Loyalty and Initiative

The manager is responsible for developing the best qualities of her staff. She wins their loyalty by gaining their admiration for the personal qualities she displays. Her example and timely comments win their loyalty to the larger organization and the cause. She develops their initiative by the policy and methods she employs in directing them in their work. She constantly encourages individual effort, taking care to commend every display of interest, innovation, ingenuity, or improvement.

She keeps the group informed of what it is trying to do so that each may understand the object of his part and seek the opportunity to do it better. She effectively tasks her personnel on what to do, not how to do it, and praises original effort and decision. By constructive criticism and explanation, she encourages her team so that each wants to do it better next time. In short, she encourages her group to observe, think, decide, and act on their decisions. The best results come from such leadership if the leader can be patient in developing these talents.

Development of the Team

How natural it is to be impatient with the supervisor who is ungainly in his early efforts. How often the manager grabs the thing and does it himself rather than wait for inexperienced hands to find the way. The manager says resentfully, "I'd rather do it myself than see John struggling with it." The manager cares more to have a certain thing done exactly as he would do it than he does for all the good that might come from the developed skill and resourcefulness of his team.

Of course, this approach is all wrong. Your way is not always the best way. One way is often as good as another, and improvements come out of the interested innovativeness of the team. Your object is to get the best efforts of your team, and good work is not done in an atmosphere of humiliation and discouragement. You must avoid the natural display of displeasure at ineffectiveness. Refrain from cutting remarks that indicate you think the team is a hopeless group of idiots.

You are developing a team and its capabilities. Constructive and innovative instincts thrive in an atmosphere of encouragement, and the opportunity to employ such instincts keeps the team cheerfully at its task. You get a double reward from this system of management—the satisfaction of seeing your subordinates grow in ability and the satisfaction of increased output or accomplishment.

Popularity

Should a manager strive for popularity with his staff? If he is brave enough to win it on his merits, it is a large element in establishing their loyalty. However, it is very easy for the inexperienced manager to have the wrong idea as to how popularity is won. He must clearly understand that it is not gained through easy-going methods, overlooking faults and neglects, or playing favorites. Such popularity is properly called *cheap*. It takes no effort to get it; it has no value once you have it. Such leadership is worse than worthless; it damages. It will be exposed at the first call for durability, by the first thing that tests the real strength of character and ability of the group. Then one of two things must happen. Either the team will fail or someone will leap to take the leadership from these weak hands and lead the team through the emergency.

We have seen this illustrated often enough in the newspapers. Some weak manager who was given authority fails in the actual tests of leadership, while some strong, quiet character steps to the front and successfully assumes the responsibilities of leadership. All executives must discover and remove these weak managers. Every manager must also study himself and his methods to ensure that both display the qualities that justify his holding the managership. In this way, the company's leadership will be ready for anything an emergency may demand.

The popularity that counts—the kind that makes employees say they would follow so-and-so through anything, that makes them brag about their leader and proud to be on his team—is founded on admiration for his real ability, on confidence in his fairness and impartiality, and on regard for his courage and strength of character. He has won this popularity by being fair and impartial to all, seeing that both privileges and extra hardships are justifiably divided among his team. He has held everyone to a strict performance of responsibility, rewarding excellence where it's due and recognizing misbehavior where it exists. Additionally, by avoiding fraudulent conduct, by showing a sincere personal interest in the welfare of his team as individuals, and through his planning and foresight—thereby saving his team unnecessary work and increasing their efficiency—he proves he really has the ability to lead them.

Appearance as to Dignity, Example, and Ability

Dignity: The manager holds his position on the assumption that out of the entire group, he is the best all-around person for the job. He must retain this reputation for excellence and should add to it by further performance. First, in appearance, that is, his worth must show in how he carries himself before his staff. The nature of the work may determine the amount of dignity that must go with the position, but in every case, the entire team must find a certain dignity in their managers that engenders respect.

A certain amount of dignity comes naturally from earnestness and sincerity of purpose. It is not a virtue to be assumed, superficial clothing to be put on for the work. It has nothing to do with arrogance or toughness. It comes simply from seeing things in their right proportion—big things big, small things small—and has more of humility than of pride. It prohibits you from patronizing your staff, from appearing to condescend to them in your dealings. And dignity does allow your sharing both their concerns and their fun. I heard a professor say, "To make a quick transition from fun to business, and to carry your team instantly with you, is the test of real dignity. The two opposites of dignity are permanent seriousness and permanent unimportance." Both extremes have a bad effect on people.

Example. Second, remember also in the matter of appearance that you are an example. Emulation is a great teacher; your staff is going to be very much as you are as their manager. Your example of optimism, promptness, loyalty to mission, cleanliness, courtesy, determination, and passion will find a response in your staff. I have seen this carried to the extent of copying the manager's manner of attire, tone in conversations, and other personal peculiarities. The power of example is an effective force and very useful in establishing loyalty.

An important example for you to give is one of purpose and interest in the work. The accomplishment of the work must appear a vital matter to you. Sluggishness and irrelevance on your part will quickly be reflected by the staff. They will equally respond to a reasonable amount of tidiness and seriousness on your part. You should appear to care so much for your work that you are uninterested in the little things that affect your comfort. If the staff see you taking advantage of your position to enjoy comforts denied to them, it encourages a state of mind that interferes with quality work.

Ability. Third, you want to impress the staff as being one who knows what is to be done in each case that arises. Let them see you make quick decisions and carry through on what you have undertaken, without changing your mind. When you figure out all the details of a certain undertaking ahead of time and carefully plan for it, you can see it through with dedication and resources that will be surprising. A few of these types of successes will establish your reputation as an effective manager.

Knowledge of Details

Your position assumes that you know the work better than any other member in your group. Generally speaking, you should be able to perform each person's part at least as well as the person, able to know when he is performing at his best, able to recognize mostly good performance to commend it, and able to correct improper methods while pointing the way to improvement. This superior knowledge gives you the self-confidence to appear before the group as their manager and to give instructions and guidelines that you know are reasonable. The staff intuitively feels and recognizes this leadership, and naturally, they will give it respect and compliance.

Of course, no manager may rationally claim to know everything or to be more skillful in every detail than certain specialists. This fact can be used to stir the pride of individuals toward greater performance and as a reason for expecting all to make suggestions for any improvements they may have thought out.

Suggestions from the Team

Suggestions from the team are to be encouraged and given fair consideration when made. If accepted, credit is to be given to the person; if rejected, he is to be told why it is not accepted. It is a mistake to feel that the manager loses standing in accepting or even listening to suggestions from his team. "Nobody can tell me how to do this job" is a narrow policy, destroying individual initiative—and it is not true anyway. The very statement shows that the manager does not fully know his job because everyone is capable of improvement, and any job is better done by combining the resourcefulness of everyone connected with it.

The Manager's Standing

The manager loses none of her standing in hearing and considering the thoughts of her staff. In the end, the decision is hers, and they all must act. It does not hurt her leadership to have to say, "I don't know. I'll have to look into that." If she finds that she has taken a wrong course, she must openly admit that she was mistaken, especially if her action was unfair to one of her staff. Mistakes are readily forgiven but not meanness or prejudice. Always remember, the staff admire fairness in their manager and demand impartiality from her.

Your staff like to feel that you are human. Above all, they will not respect a pretender. It is hopeless to try to fake when you do not know. Someone will know and expose you, and away goes the respect of your staff.

Asking the Team's Opinions

I have known successful managers who make it a rule to ask, whenever one of their team members comes to them with some question or dilemma, "What do you think about it? What would you advise doing?" The team member has most likely been thinking about this for a while before it was presented. If it is a question about the work, he probably has a solution in mind, and this may be his way of getting it considered.

By asking his opinion, you encourage his personal interest in overall success, solicit his cooperation, allow self-expression, and gain time for consideration of your answer while he is presenting his. It is often a particularly good way to handle some negligence in duty and responsibility on the part of your staff member. Ask him what he would do, if he were the manager, with a person who committed the same offense. It is astonishing how this makes him realize the whole situation, which he probably had not thought of before. Nine times out of ten, he will suggest a more severe re-direct than you would give, and he'll come out of the experience a much more responsive member of the staff than before.

A Representative of Authority

The immediate manager of a department is to his team the direct representative of authority, which holds them to their tasks. The manager reminds all of the company's purpose and policy, which must inspire their endeavors and direct innovation. The team will largely get its impressions of the impartiality and fairness of all company authority from that displayed by their manager; they will critique the worthiness of purpose and policy from his passion and loyalty and will evaluate overall efficiency by his daily actions.

Executives considered all this when they selected you as a manager; it is now for you to consider it constantly in dealing with your team. The more ignorant a team member, the more important that you treat him fairly and prudently. It is up to you to make him a comfortable, useful employee and happy citizen. Your example can save him from believing that authority is unfair or the organization unworthy of his loyalty.

The Head of the Family

A quality manager is always a jealous guardian of the personal rights of his personnel. It is only over his dead body that unfairness is done to any of his team. He is their champion in every contact with the larger organization, and they look up to him for it. The team instinct is one of strong self-protection. In the innumerable groupings of the business world, the individual chooses to give his loyalty to those teams he believes offer him the best protection. The manager takes advantage of this psychological fact when he makes his team realize that he is constantly on the lookout for their interests.

He may be stern with them himself (in a parental way), but he allows no one else to do so. He sees that they receive what they have earned. If hardship must be endured, he sees that it is endured reasonably and shares it with them. He fights for their fair name and the full recognition of their worth. If one of his personnel has trouble, it becomes his trouble until it is adjusted. He establishes the feeling that it is a family matter and he is the head of the family.

Likewise, his team will reward him by taking a keen interest in his welfare as the head of their family. And in the end, his personnel come to speak of it as *our* team—not Smith's or Brown's but *our* group—because each realizes that his interests are equal with the others. Until his team speaks of the department as *ours* rather than *his*, the manager has not influenced the cooperative spirit he desires.

The Team Spirit

Any team of individuals working together for a common purpose will unconsciously establish a team spirit of some kind. The wise manager knows that success mainly depends on what this spirit will be, so he makes an effort to ensure it is a helpful one.

By getting to know your staff and "how they feel about it," you keep in close touch with the spirit that runs through them all. Suggestions here and there do much to build the team in the direction it should go and to make each feel a valued member. When you have learned this spirit well, you can count on your staff to respond in a certain way to demands or desires. Team spirit becomes a tool in your hand for getting results. In a time of adversity or stress, you play on this spirit to arouse new energy or endurance. Team spirit will make them endure, challenge, and tough it out far beyond normal accomplishment.

So, the successful manager is constantly on the lookout for ways to build up this splendid spirit in his team. By word and deed, he fosters the spirit of putting things across and never being defeated, which will carry them through to success when called. His team comes to realize that what he requires of them is always reasonable and efficient. They find he is always considering their welfare before his and taking great pride in the team's success. They come to realize that while he directs their work, making it interesting for them, he will never accept failure for them or himself. Rather, he insists on leading through to successful accomplishment. It is possible to establish so strong a team spirit for doing quality work that they will correct the lazybones and expose the ones adding no value as being unfit for membership on the team.

Such results are possible to the successful manager in direct proportion to his knowledge of his job and his ability to perform the work with proficiency and good time management. Business professionals typically detest inefficiency. They become critical, destructive in their remarks, and finally disgusted under a mediocre manager who wastes their time and efforts, hesitates over decisions, and wonders whether to act. Additionally, if he does not have the tools and material on hand, if he fails to select the right person for the task, and if he delays work while he argues with a member of his team, such a manager will never build up any good spirit.

Work for the Manager

Not all managers will be sure and confident in all matters of management. However, by looking ahead, planning and preparing for each new task, thinking and working overtime when required, they can fit themselves for each task and lead their teams with such efficient direction that they will almost seem to be a hero. Of course, this means work for the manager, and effort must increase as one ascends the ladder of promotion. The manager who is half as good as he should be in his position is usually profiting the company more than his pay grade would indicate. His task is not an easy one. The motives which hold the manager to his job are the ambition for accomplishment, pride in success, and the joy of meeting respectable responsibility—not the enjoyment of an easy position.

Where Leadership Shows

As we watch a skillful manager directing his staff through a project, tools and material all on hand, every person moving resourcefully, all the parts working smoothly toward the result, how natural it is to shout, "What teamwork!" and "What a manager!" But out of years of experience, I tell you that this manager seems so successful because he previously sat down and planned out how to handle this special project. He made efforts to see to it ahead of time that everything was prepared to start the work.

His superior leadership shows not in the work he is currently doing but in work he did beforehand, in building up the discipline and teamwork of his staff and in preparing them to handle this special project professionally. That is why he may now appear so quietly confident in himself and his staff. The real task for leadership is matching self, people, and team ahead of time so they may work smoothly to the best advantage without waste or friction.

Assuring the Confidence of the Staff

It is a common fault of managers to take too much for granted and assume that their staff understands conditions without bothering to explain them. Remember that a person cannot provide quality work if his mind is concealing fear or distrust, or if he is questioning his rights, duties, or the assurance of receiving fair, firm, and impartial treatment. Confidence in and knowledge of the conditions under which he works will keep his mind free from these disturbing invaders.

Perhaps nothing can do more to free his mind than to provide him with a copy of the rules and regulations that clearly define the administration and controls; the rights, duties, and mutual relations of all members; and mainly the method by which each may file a grievance for an incursion of his rights or impartial treatment. We all know that, in business, the staffer's distrust of the impartiality and honesty of his manager is often justified, and we can see the advantages of letting him know his rights and giving him easy access to a higher authority. The enormity of modern organizations has too often made management forget its responsibility in the matter of correction and fair treatment of employees.

Assuring Fairness

The possession of authority makes a successful manager consider the rights of others, so as not to do a severe unfairness. In contrast, authority's effect on an average manager is far different; he often becomes selfish, mean, and arrogant; indifferent to the feelings and rights of others; and partial to favoritism for selfish reasons. He denies fairness and forfeits his right to leadership. Such managers are often the cause of serious personnel issues and are always the cause of a loss of productivity.

By deception and dishonesty, they may conceal these qualities from executives for a long time while they continue to neglect the most humane policies of the organization. For this reason, when dilemmas show on any team, seek the source in the substandard leadership of their manager. Fairness is the reason successful managers hold training and often check on the equal opportunity of their staff. They make it clearly understood that every team member has ready access to a higher authority for the presentation of any grievance.

The Joy of Doing Work Well

A manager naturally takes delight in a job well done. He gets genuine pleasure from doing well whatever he does with his hands. The joys from satisfactory execution of work are the result of both instinct and system, which are the best ways for obtaining results if the manager knows how to use them.

When you see a manager taking no interest in his work and not trying to obtain positive results, perhaps even purposely performing poorly, you can be sure that something is fundamentally wrong. Some stronger instinct has been stirred whose strength prevents attention to his work. Our strongest instincts are those of self-protection, and one of these may be causing trouble. If conditions are such as to make the manager fearful of his welfare, life, or equality, self-protection instincts are likely to overcome, or at least confuse, the instinct to do well. So, we may expect greater results only under a system which assures fairness and impartiality and under a manager who honestly practices them.

Appeal to the Productive Instincts

A common complaint at the end of the day is that the manager is too tired to do anything more. This is true. However, it is not because of the amount of work he has done; rather, the faltering motivation is because of the small amount of interest and ambition he has put into his job. Most managers are happiest in doing hard work and quality work if they take the right approach to it. It is the lack of trust between executives and managers that denies managers the privilege of giving full attention to their productive instincts.

A daily standard of mediocrity harms the character of those capable, ambitious managers who work as malingerers, instead of giving their best. No wonder these managers are tired at night and have no heart for outside social interests. They are working in an environment which saps their energy and cuts their self-respect. You may see this evidenced in their dull faces as they continue their jobs. Managers often become more interested in the success of their organizations and their responsibility when no danger threatens, when no issues are at stake. A clever manager may appeal to the productive instincts as to make them dominate the self-protective ones.

Depending on a Staffer

You can make a member of your staff strongly feel that you are trusting him to play fair in a certain matter. If you leave it up to him, his sense of confidence and team-player attitude will make him feel that he owes it to you to do well. This is a strong influence on demeanor—too strong to be used constantly. It may easily become troublesome to ordinary others, who generally want more freedom from the pressures of conscience. The point is to use it only in special cases and obtain its positive effect both in results attained and on the growth of the staffer's character. When you do use it, do so naturally and easily without too much hassle or talking and certainly without putting him on the spot publicly. There should be no outward question of your confidence—it is to be understood as so certain that you do not have to talk about it.

Ownership and Self-Expression

Ownership and self-expression are two strong instincts of which successful managers take advantage. The manager should be made to feel that he has a personal interest in the job he is doing and that in doing it, he is using his knowledge, skills, and abilities. The manager watches for the opportunity and drops a remark to show that he sees how well a member of his team has performed, and no harm is done if others overhear. The manager is similarly careful to speak of it as Smith's job, to praise the way *Smith* handled it, and to commend the excellent condition of Smith's tools or resources. In doing so, he encourages everyone to do their work and receive credit accordingly.

Ownership and self-expression must also carry meaning for you as the manager. Growing these traits in your staff will, in turn, cause them to resent it when they find themselves doing useless work, wasting time or energy, or even approaching failure as a result of your poor judgment, hesitation in making decisions, and lack of planning. You must, therefore, know your job and carefully prepare yourself to handle its details.

Knowing the Purpose of Work

Successful managers understand that before their team can put its best efforts to work, they must know the why behind the task. Purpose is the guiding motive in all of life, and the team will instinctively seek the purpose in all its efforts. Upon finding it and believing in it, the team will naturally give purpose its best endeavors. One of the greatest faults in handling work is not making known what the team is doing or why.

A person must have some interest in his task before he can put much heart or intelligence into it. It is quite possible in assigning a task to make sure that the person understands the object of it, what role it plays, and its importance in the overall work of the team. Then, no matter how simple his part may be, as the person works, he builds a mental picture of the completed whole, see his part fitting into it, and make his part perfect. Meanwhile, the ability to clearly define the purpose of the work reflects favorably on the manager as it signals that he has a clear conception of this thing and can cut to the chase in explaining each part.

To most efficiently start new work, a new project, or new policy, assemble the entire team and explain what you and they together are trying to accomplish. Let them know how they are organized for it and the part each is to take. Clear explanation may serve as inspiration or it may appeal to their reason. Do not let it ever be said of your staff that they are working in ignorance of what they are trying to accomplish. Do not exclude them from putting intelligent interest and cooperation into their respective parts.

Relationship between Manager and Team

The relationship which should exist between the manager and his team is a difficult thing to explain accurately. It depends largely on the manager's personality, and accordingly, each must work the details out for himself. This is almost always a matter of difficulty and embarrassment for beginners, who are apt to go to an unhappy extreme either in surrounding themselves with an atmosphere of isolation and dictatorship or in showing too much familiarity. Let them first remember that the manager is not a tyrant or dictator but the leader of his former companions. While this position puts responsibility and authority in his hands, it also calls for a certain restraint on the perfect freedom of his relations with the others. A sense of leadership and protocol must remain in his demeanor, which they will recognize, making it natural for them to respect him and follow his instructions. He may be friendly but must not be a fraternizer. He should be courteous and thoughtful for their interests but never patronizing.

A successful manager is always courteous to those in junior positions. He has no anxiety about his prestige and is quietly at ease in dealing with his team. The manager who bullies his team is showing that he does not have much experience in exerting authority. The true spirit of America believes in the dignity of labor. The manager and his team are all companions in business and labor, and each shows respect for the ability and accomplishment of the other.

That is the spirit of the relationship between manager and team by which he is to adjust his conduct. You can see how this team spirit can be offended by patronizing or displays of either arrogant authority or immature actions. Both team and manager are each entitled to the serious consideration of the other. Each part shows respect for the other. Successful managers understand that you are all on the same team. It happens that you are at the pitcher's mound now, but someday each one of you will have your turn to hit the ball.

Reception of New Staff

The ultimate success of a new staff member joining a team depends on the things that are in him. But much can be done to accelerate this success. It has been the practice throughout the years to embarrass or humiliate the newcomer to bring out what is inside of him. Today, this is no longer an approved practice. Instead, better results are reaped more quickly through encouragement and by showing a person *how* rather than knocking him over the head for not knowing.

This becomes another care for the manager, who must see that each new staff member gets off on the right start. You can be sure that most new staff members want to do well. Encourage them along that line and try to prevent the occurrence of anything which will switch them to the opposite track. To most of them, an early display of your friendly personal interest in how they are coming along will be a great help and incentive to perform better.

They will not understand many things and will fret over both real and imaginary dilemmas. This is your chance to establish a relationship of confidence in which they form the habit of bringing these difficulties to you for a solution, instead of letting them fester in their minds until they act as deterrents to the good desire for work. This gives you many opportunities for improving team dynamics and may someday be the means of clearing up real grievances, which might otherwise lead to serious trouble.

The new staff member's future depends largely on the start he gets, on his first impressions of the team and policies of the organization, and on the early habits he forms. The smarter he finds the organization to be, the more pride he will take in belonging to it. The closer attention he is forced to give to the exact performance of small details, the sooner he will get into the habit of doing things exactly right and the sooner he will become a helpful member of the team. You can teach new tricks to new staff members much more easily than you can to old ones whose well-formed habits you must break before you can insert the new ones. New staff members are an asset to a successful manager because he can influence them to become the kind of professionals he knows the organization needs.

Take Time to Hear Your Team

The manager must have time to listen to his team. He must not be too busy to take on any matter brought to him for consideration. It is easy to look important and say, "I don't have the time," but each time the manager does this, he drives one more nail in the coffin of team cohesiveness. Chances are, he declines the interview because he fears that he does not know the answer. It is far better to take that chance, to make the person feel that he was right in coming to you and then listen to his proposition, even if in the end you must admit that you do not know.

You must *make* time if you want the loyal cooperation of your team. I know a successful manager who was given an unproductive department, yet he managed to properly organize and lead them to great results. The first thing he did was to place a sign outside his office door: "I have the time to hear you." It is much harder to get your team to give you the honest, timely expressions you need if you give the impression you can't be bothered by too many of them.

The busiest manager can and should arrange his activities and policy so that every team member knows he can personally meet if the occasion warrants it. Inform your team to bring any dilemmas they are having directly to you. You'll watch the difficulties rapidly diminish, and your time will be well repaid in added productivity.

Conversing with Your Team

The manager has much to consider when conversing with his team members. He may not talk enough, or he may talk too much. He must explain to the team the mission, organization, and policy of any new undertaking. By doing so, he gets better results and saves a lot of talking later. On the other hand, a reputation for constantly blabbing and preaching would essentially ruin him. A manager should observe the rule not to speak unless he has something worth saying and that nothing is worth saying unless it is worth being heard.

The habit of speaking without requiring the close attention of the ones who are supposed to be interested is bad business and causes confusion and misunderstandings later. Many managers are guilty of it and expect to repeat their instructions over and over before they are understood. This is partly their fault and partly that of the listeners—but the managers are responsible for both sides.

In the first place, the manager must speak directly to the point. If he does not have this ability, he must daily teach himself. He must first think of what he has to say and exactly how he is going to say it. Then, he must say it and stop. He will not talk as much, but what he says will go further. Many managers are unaccustomed to saying things that count, and they become embarrassed and confused when they find themselves the focus of close attention. The successful manager regards holding the close attention of the team as the second and equally important part of his responsibility in conversing successfully.

Demanding the Attention of All

When you have something to say, to one person or many, be sure first to obtain their full attention. Then insist on maintaining it while you are speaking. We so often see the impossible situation of a manager making remarks, which he considers important, while his personnel are giving attention to other matters, even engaging in inside conversations. When you must speak to your team, gather them in one location, in front of you, where you can see all their faces, and as near to you as practical so you may speak in a conversational tone, if possible. You can now be sure that your points are heard because everyone is near you. If an interruption occurs, immediately stop talking until everyone can give their attention again. If your remarks are for everybody, everybody should hear them, and *you* are responsible that they do hear them. Make that a rule, stick to it yourself, and you should have no worry.

Conversing with Individuals

In conversing with an individual, try to be so clear and definite that you will not have to repeat it. Let it be understood that you expect a level of attention that will render repetition unnecessary. Of course, you sometimes must deal with a mind so untrained in concentration that it cannot take things in and retain them, and you will have to be patient in making yourself understood. The most selfish type of mind is the one that keeps thinking while you are speaking of what it is going to say when it gets a chance. This type gives your remarks just enough attention to note when a pause comes so it may begin to speak.

Yet, this kind of thinking cannot be tolerated in business. The art of listening is a valuable one, and everyone should develop the habit of concentrated attention to what is being said. It is particularly valuable in receiving instructions. In fact, promotion is more likely to come to the manager of whom his executive can report, "He gives his full attention when you tell him anything, and you never have to repeat yourself."

Example Is Better than Talk

In the line of not talking too much, I think it is vital to remember that if the manager wants passion and interest in doing one's work, he must arouse his team by example rather than by words. As you know, actions speak louder than words. You cannot motivate your team by telling them that you want them there. You must daily display the follow-the-leader life force and put so much cheerful energy and vitality into your work that it is contagious. By powerful direction, joyful recommendation, possibly a bit of competition, and, most of all, by example, you motivate your team unconsciously and hold them there until the task is done. Then, you may all talk about how good it was and share the credit.

Talks by the Big Chief

The manager of any organization will get far better results if he makes occasion for assembling all his supervisors to talk to them about policies, his plans, and how things are going in general. The manager who denies close relationship to his supervisors, who does not take them into his confidence to let them know his plans and how he proposes to carry them out, creates the suspicion either that he is not sure of himself in his job or that his plans and purposes are ineffective.

The successful manager does not fear scrutiny and does seek cooperation and recommendations. He makes himself the captain of a team whose members cooperate intelligently for the team's success. For this purpose, he brings them together in a body where, shoulder to shoulder, they feel their camaraderie in a common cause and get inspiration from their captain's leadership as they absorb passion from the presentation of his expectations and plans. All are filled with a common purpose and return to their tasks better tailored and more highly determined to play their part to the overall success of the organization.

The most successful project managers took time and effort to assemble their team before a major project to explain, in person, the general plan of the coming action and the exact part of each member. With no effort at eloquent appeal to passion or devotion, simply a recognition of the team's ability and willingness to do is its entire part, this approach has never failed to work, and it will work well for all managers.

Managing of Work

The manager's job is one of supervision and direction. It is his business to see that each member of the team does his part for the overall benefit of the organization and to know the individual capacities of his supervisors so that he can assign the right one to each task. This, as do all the other duties of leadership, requires him to be continually watching the individual performances of his supervisors, commending, correcting, and coordinating their efforts. This prohibits his taking part in doing the work himself, not because to do so would be beneath his dignity but because becoming involved in doing the actual work would distract his attention from the duties of managing, thus permitting many things to go on without his knowledge.

There are always some supervisors on the team who need to be held accountable for their work. If the manager allows them to get away with dodging their parts of the task, it will irritate the others. The manager is responsible for the spirit of teamwork, which requires that each supervisor feel sure all others are equally faithful in doing their part. Therefore, the manager must see to it that they are. Of course, conditions may arise, as when the task is unfamiliar or unusually difficult, when the manager may jump in for a minute to show the supervisors how or to set the pace—but he should never put himself in as an actual performer of their work.

Choosing the Right People for Tasks

The duties of a manager constantly require her to be picking some member of her staff to perform a task. In the minds of her staff, this is always a test of both her ability and fairness—and she wants to prove that she has both. She does this by picking the right person for the job, not only because the person is the best qualified but also because, everything considered, it is best for the team.

This process requires the manager to know the knowledge, skills, and abilities of her team and to keep track of their conduct and work performance. The manager who desires her tasks to be completed must always choose in a way that will avoid the possibility of insubordination. The manager must not fail in fairness by putting extra work on the more willing. Sometimes, it may be prudent to choose the lazy or moody ones for the extra work, putting the emphasis on cheerfulness. In this way, the manager proves she has a sense of fairness and an ability to run the team.

Cheerfulness, a Responsibility

A team cannot perform their best work in an atmosphere of pessimism. Flexible muscles, alert minds, formidable energy, and enduring stamina come from a cheerful state of mind and happy hearts. It is unfortunate if the team does not contain at least one resolute soul who will joke and have fun through hardships and great accomplishments alike. Some managers sacrifice cheerfulness by asserting abrupt, inconsiderate, and dominating control as to keep their team uncomfortable and heavy-hearted, discouraged with themselves and the work and uninterested in results. These managers create an atmosphere of impenetrable unhappiness and then expect the impossible in demanding the best performance of work.

Cheerfulness and hopefulness must always come from the manager— no possible hardship or obstacle may justify his failing to radiate these helpful qualities. They glow from a character too strong and resourceful to be overcome by any obstacle. You will find instances when it will test your courage, strength, and energy to do this, but you must give the complete force of your cheerful dominance to overcome adversity and lead them through to a happy conclusion.

Letting off Steam Is Permissible

A certain amount of letting off steam seems good, but it all depends on who does it and how it is done. You may ignore it, make light of it, and even sometimes get a good laugh out of it, but it is doubtful you may ever indulge in it yourself in the presence of the team. If the loose talk speaks of disloyalty, however, then you may not tolerate it because it will undermine the team's morale. Know the members on your team so you can know how to take their comments and how to prevent anything like real disloyalty. You must dissuade members from losing their responsibility in favor of acting immaturely, like children, with such comments. And always consider the actual feelings behind their words as they converse.

I recall the situation of a colleague whose team just barely completed the first part of a two-part software project. The other team could not meet the standards, so my colleague's team was tasked by the senior vice president to complete the second part of the project. He sat complacently smoking while his bewildered team let off steam and told each other the terrible things that would take place before they would do the other team's part.

He knew his team and let them rumble it out, and when the time was up, not one of them hesitated to follow his direction to go back into the building to get started. In his place, a hot-headed young software engineer could easily have started a rebellion. Such situations require a level head and a knowledge of the true spirit of the team—and are interesting tests of one's qualifications as a manager.

Loyalty by Example

One of the basic things the manager must develop in his team is loyalty—and loyalty not to him and the team alone but to the entire organization. To this end, the manager does much by the power of his example in cheerfully carrying out the instructions from executives. If you are told to do something distasteful, do not try for cheap acceptance by saying to the team, "The executives ordered me to do this, and we have to get it done." Accept the full responsibility of your position and lead your team loyally and unquestioningly through the work. Your team is a member of the larger organizational team and should be a team player therein as loyally and intensely as you want the individuals to play their parts on your team. Awaken their pride in doing their part well, taking interest in the success of the organization, and believing in the ability of the manager.

How to Encourage Suggestions

An organization that accepted the idea to value the suggestions from their staff tried to buy them off by initiating a bi-weekly prize contest, rewarding those giving suggestions. It was their notion that for a prize of fifty-dollar gift cards, they would get the suggestions needed. This method missed all appreciation of the fundamental principles involved and ended in a travesty.

Successful managers want suggestions that spring naturally from the interest and partnership they have fostered in the organization. They want ideas for improvement which come to team members as they go about their work, thinking how it might be improved or how the team might get greater results. The only encouragement the team needs is the atmosphere of partnership and a manager who has sense enough to give their suggestions fair consideration. The manager who does not have the time or patience to listen to suggestions can never influence the best efforts of the team and is doing the organization actual damage.

Every member of the team should feel confident that his suggestion will be fairly considered and, if his idea has real value, that he will be given full credit up to the highest levels. You must take the team member in person to a higher authority and have him explain his idea. This makes his importance very real to him. If the team member is called before the board of directors to explain the details of some process improvement he has suggested, nothing can do more to establish a sense of partnership. By appreciating their value, you can take advantage of every opportunity to increase the team's interest in the work and their sense of cooperation.

Advantage of Ambition

The manager should consider ambition, both in connection with his career and in dealing with his team. He should feel that he can be promoted as far as his genuine ability permits—successful managers are desired at the top. Managers must realize that selfish ambition will never win, that it is only by being a team player and working for the best interests of the entire organization that one can receive his executive's recommendation for promotion. The unselfish ambition of a manager improves both his chances for promotion and the work of the team.

It is mostly true throughout the business industry that the boundless stream of intelligence, innovation, and creativity flows from the bottom up, not from the top down, and that the top is continually being recruited from the bottom—as managers daily graduate from the classes of supervisors. The latter is so common that it is frequently overlooked. It is a fact so characteristic of our millennial organizations and so helpful a thought in times of displeasure and discouragement that it should be emphasized and frequently recalled.

Never Deny an Earned Promotion

An earned promotion should never be denied a team member when her opportunity arrives, simply because her manager thinks that she is the "go-to" leader. As unfair as that is, it is often done and always at the cost of the team spirit. Very few team members in business are so important to their positions that they cannot be replaced—and often to surprising benefit. No matter what efforts are necessary to train the team member's replacement, it is far better to let her go than it is to keep her and lower the morale of the entire team by showing that your selfishness or laziness is going to stand in the way of a deserved promotion. An excellent rule, which often prevents this situation, is for each team member in the organization to have at least one other who is qualified to take her place.

How to Get Promotion

It is not practical to list all the ways to get promoted. The internet, magazine articles, and business journals are always providing suggestions. But here are a few general hints: A manager does not get promoted by bragging about his abilities but by making his value conspicuous. You may be sure that executives are always seeking the managers who can produce and that great results will catch their eye. Attempt each task optimistically, and above all, make it clear that your one big interest is the success of the organization. One thing that so often denies promotion to a quality manager is this statement by his executive, "Miller is a very sharp manager, but he thinks nine times for Miller and once for the company." This is too bad, as the same amount of work and ability unselfishly directed might have led him forward.

The Joy of Accomplishment

The manager's enjoyment in doing things well is the motive for accomplishment; he has true pleasure in seeing a task completed. Most of us know colleagues who are ruled by this passion, who are so consumed with doing something that they are not interested in anything else until they have completed it. One of America's most successful businesspersons once replied when asked what he considered the best thing in life, "The satisfaction that comes from accomplishment." This may be enjoyed by every manager, no matter his background because it is the satisfaction derived from the accomplishment of daily work tasks.

The manager may often appeal to this instinct to increase accomplishment. It helps explain the advantage of letting staffers know what they are doing as they work, especially letting them know from time to time what they have accomplished toward the overall result. This is the reason that the placement of progress charts does so much to stir interest in factory and shop work and is another reason for including the staffer in a knowledge of the general progress of the entire organization.

The manager is supposed to have a purpose, a goal in business, but he gains much satisfaction en route from the successful completion of each of the small steps that bring him nearer to the goal. The day feels effective when he has taken even one step. So, the manager may encourage staffers and assure their continued efforts by showing them where they have made successful progress toward the desired end.

Indifference and Discouragement

Indifference and discouragement come from failure. They can even come from what *seems* like failure when continuous efforts show no results or from growing weary through the constant repetition of the same task, without variety or the stimulation of new ideas. The manager must combat these adversaries by introducing other thoughts to replace them. He must encourage the discouraged and interest those who are bored. He may often stimulate interest in even monotonous work by commenting on the perfection of its execution and the amount of daily output. It is possible to relieve the monotony of long hours at the same tedious machine by letting two people alternate tasks—if it can be done without offending proprietorship, which makes one resent having another touch his machine. Here is the manager's chance for imagination. He knows what is needed; it is up to him to supply it.

Impartiality and Fairness

Impartiality and fairness are commonly considered fundamental in successfully leading teams, and yet, managers do not often consider them. The business environment demands fairness and gives its best response only in that atmosphere. No matter our personal beliefs, we have to recognize that our best advances come as we realize how positively people react to fairness and decent treatment.

It has been said that 90 percent of civilization is good and will do good when confidence is shown in their good intentions. Thus, the working rules for an organization should be made to fit the majority rather than the 10 percent minority.

This same attitude of irrelevance (to the well-being of the stellar-performing staff) to direct the lazy performers is to be found in every business. The point is that better results may often be obtained by showing confidence in good intentions, allowing more freedom of action, and influencing the unkinder attitudes through instruction, removal, and encouraging emulation of their stellar-performing teammates. The manager should remember that success for the organization is accomplished by the ability to awaken an attitude that makes the staff want to give 100 percent results. It is not shown by control through random methods.

The manager will experience various situations in which he must show impartiality and fairness. It is impossible to anticipate them, but you may encounter them successfully by a continuing determination not to act impatiently and to judge each case fairly with the thought of how it will affect everyone. In doing so, you will arrive at the best solutions. Always consider the Golden Rule about "doing unto others" and remember that your final decisions must have in mind character development and the team's correction.

Excess Energy

At times a team member has so much energy that they are unable to expend enough of it on the daily routine—and the excess often gets them into trouble. A successful manager accommodates them with enough hard work and freedom to keep them comfortably engaged, while the average manager blindly reprimands their failures without effort at remedy, giving the team member a reputation as a troublemaker or as insignificant.

These team members are capable of tremendous efforts for quality work if properly directed. Competition for executive positions can be a perfect outlet for energy, resulting in an often-brilliant performance to the delight of their manager. These team members found in the demands of duties and responsibilities enough to engage all their excess energies, and because of this, they were able to outperform their colleagues.

Giving your staff work to keep them out of trouble is a wise saying. The trick is to select the person who may be getting into trouble, awaken his self-importance by finding some part of his personality to praise and rely on, and then put him in charge of a group or small project. Nine times out of ten, he will react to this responsibility by giving an unusual performance. The difficulty is to find the opportunity to encourage a seeming troublemaker so that he may win a chance at character development and promotion.

Courage, Fear, and Self-Control

In many fields of business activity, a manager is likely to be called upon to meet emergencies requiring a level head and a courageous heart. Some managers shy away from assuming the responsibilities of leadership because they lack the courage and confidence when the test comes. It would be helpful for them to understand something about fearful emotions, why they come, and how they can be controlled.

We may assume that all managers feel fear. The self-protective instincts are perhaps the strongest of all our instincts. Fear is the instinctive warning of the nearness of danger, urging us to take steps to meet the danger, to take action. Then we forget the fear, as it normally disappears when we have entered the action.

A developed mind, character, and determined purpose combine to enable us to avoid showing fear or letting it improperly influence our actions. No one would willingly follow a manager who lacked a courageous character, nor could a manager hope to carry on successfully if he was self-conscious of his ethical weakness. So, both the manager and team must have confidence that the manager possesses courage and force of character so that he will be self-controlled and capable of calm, reasonable decisions in the crises of his work.

The manager establishes this confidence by the self-control and good judgment evident in the administration of the smaller emergencies he meets daily. If he becomes excited over small things or shouts and screams because something goes wrong, he is not only failing in self-control but is also making his team question his business character and his ability to meet a real situation. A new manager should train himself in self-control during difficult circumstances; he should even seek situations which test his nerve and judgment, rather than avoid trouble as the average manager does by quietly slipping away.

Control by Power of Example

It is the manager's job to be calm in an emergency, relaxed and humorous in the face of hardships, and composed and even self-controlled in the face of danger. Your team will emulate your mental attitude. In danger, like an active shooter situation, your team will watch your actions, even facial expression, for reassurance. It is then that you drop some casual remark, "Remember your training," and do any simple thing naturally, showing that you are at ease and confident in these abnormal circumstances, allowing your team to reclaim their uncertain confidence as they feel that you are not afraid.

In a time of unavoidable hardship, you must avoid displaying annoyance or impatience. Your acceptance of necessary conditions will unconsciously lead to theirs and save damage to pride, camaraderie, and common loyalty shared by the team. In an emergency, you must show perfect self-control—not grumble, kick, and curse out everyone. Remember that your conduct will determine that of your team. If you are excited, they will be even more excited. An emergency calls for the most accurate, determined, and self-controlled work, and if your heart has jumped into your throat and made your voice quiver and your ideas confused (and this will happen to the best of managers), nothing but disaster may result if you communicate this to your team.

You will gain success in the end if you the take time to be calm and self-assured. Give your directions clearly and concisely. Directions given in such a manner are a great comfort to the team and guarantee strong, intelligent execution. To begin shouting excited, misguided instructions in an emergency is one of the most characteristic failures of inexperienced leadership. Train yourself in unflustered assurance by mastering self-control in any given situation. Be confident and then calmly give directions to your team.

You can train for this by thoroughly reading this book that you may acquire the habits of successful managers for knowing what to do in an emergency and doing it with calm assurance. In any business accident or emergency, generally you'll find some worthy bystander whose mind has acted instantaneously, who has jumped in and done the right thing. Question your mental processes to learn why you were not the manager and try to qualify next time.

Decision

It is characteristic of a successful manager to make good decisions, which do not have to be changed, and to stick to them. In contrast, it is characteristic of bold ignorance to make quick decisions that are usually wrong. Of course, quick decisions are preferable if they are correct. At times, the manager may take time to weigh his topic before deciding. In many cases, it is even best that he first takes time to consult his staff.

In every case, however, he must ultimately decide on the course of action, clearly publicize it as his decision, and have the strength of character to carry it out without showing hesitation or indecision. The lazy manager is one who cannot make up his mind; the average manager is the one who is influenced by the last person who spoke to him, hesitating and changing at each new thought or development presented. If you have any of those inclinations, eliminate them by assessing yourself in making decisions. By practice in the small matters, develop the ability to grasp the important facts of a situation, to arrive promptly at a decision, and to stick to it despite unimportant matters that may come along to make a change appear better.

Value of Thinking

The more you think about the details and possibilities of your job, the more you keep your mind on your work, the better you will be prepared to make good decisions quickly. "Because I am always thinking about it" was Napoleon's answer when asked how he was able to make such prompt, accurate decisions in the art of war. We teach all of our supervisors to be constantly thinking about what to do if a crisis appears in any of the various situations he meets and to keep his mind prepared to make his decision quickly. Once they become manager, those who continue to think of the business and prepare themselves mentally to meet daily demands will do best. It is the unexpected thing, the element of surprise, that catches a manager off guard, Without preparation, the surprise will bring uncertainty and indecision.

A manager should be found so resourceful and sure of her judgment that she can successfully meet all events with a quick decision. She can do so by carefully planning her time for certain tasks and then by making quick decisions during their execution. However, to maintain this reputation, she must also acquire the habit of giving thought to her work, not only in anticipation of certain jobs but continually as the work progresses. The mind that does not have to be recalled from a mid-day vacation to the Cayman Islands will grasp the important details of a new situation more quickly and accurately than one who was not prepared when the unexpected happened.

Personal Pride

The successful manager expects his team to give to the demands of their duties and responsibilities; therefore, he builds up their pride: in themselves, in what they are doing, and in the organization. This pride is largely established by looking for cases of greater accomplishment and praising them.

Once developed, pride becomes an influence on which the manager may appeal successfully for better performance, better results, and persistent endurance of hardship. It will not instantly happen, but it will come from the performance of quality work that has been recognized as such and in an acceptable feeling of capability and worth. Do not expect to get it by simply announcing to your team that they are the best. Communicate a true regard for their worth through praising their excellent performance and making fitting remarks to outsiders that some of them may overhear. Find something in which they excel and boast about it discreetly. If possible, make an occasion to demonstrate their ability publicly. If your organization can receive a reputation for excellence, it will become more excellent. Stellar performers will seek to join the team; its personnel will improve; and it will continue to grow even better.

Pride in the Organization

Pride in the organization is a tremendous influence on keeping staff on their toes. It makes them keep each other's standards up—and the manager will reap the rewards for having established it. It's a delight to see staff developing the self-accountability you have hoped for and the cooperation in teamwork you've fostered as both add tremendous value to the organization.

Every manager should always strive to stimulate this type of respectable pride. Make practical use of your knowledge so that your team takes delight in doing things well and having their excellence recognized. The excellence of the individual should be reflected in the reputation of the team. Out of their mental development, grow self-respect, commendable self-importance, and assurance that strengthens individual character—all elements of the larger organization's spirit.

Competition Affecting Individuals

The instinct of rivalry or competition, which makes team members strive to excel among their cohorts, is another of the manager's instruments. This is so powerful a motive that it must be used with judgment. Once tossed in a real contest, most individuals are likely to do anything to win. A colleague told me of an instance where he discovered one of his team members cheating on a proficiency examination. The staffer was open in admitting to my colleague that he had used a cheat sheet, and when asked why, he innocently replied, "I heard you say we must beat last year's scores, and I was trying to help." He was so honest that my colleague had to admit that the fault was half his and did not reprimand him.

As a rule, what we want from our team is high performance, but you must judge the case fairly before introducing the spirit of contest. You must not be using it forever to keep the team under some form of control but only on meaningful occasions. You would not want an individual to be driving himself continuously to capacity. Therefore, use judgment to protect against individual hurt as well as to keep the essence of competition fresh for use on real occasions.

Team Competitions

Competition between teams engaged in similar events will not only increase results but will also provide the huge advantage of bringing the individuals of each team into close cooperation. It provides a clearer understanding of teamwork. However, if your team competes with another in the organization, it must play fair at being a member of the larger team. Rules of cooperation and loyalty among your team apply but so do rules of fairness toward the other. You may not do anything for your team that would harm the other team or degrade it. Building up team spirit by negative or profane slurs against the other will be expensive in terms of wasted time if a future project links the two teams together in the same team and each finds himself dependent on the cooperation of the other for success. A confident, "Sure, he's good, but we can beat him," is the true professional attitude for contests within an organization.

The Wellbeing of Your Team

When looking after the wellbeing of your team, two opposing considerations are to be kept in mind. You must build up their self-respect, initiative, individual responsibility, and self-determination while never patronizing, coddling, or treating them like children. On the other hand, you must recognize the individual characteristics of the people on the team and know when to shift individual responsibility to the team without giving up your authority. The need for oversight is true in every event, and the manager must be on the lookout to see that his team does the things necessary for their comfort and welfare.

Physical wellbeing is particularly necessary for out-of-doors jobs, as in engineering and construction. The manager may be too tired or inexperienced to see to it himself that each worker has a comfortable place to rest, but the successful manager knows that the work of the next day will depend on the rest his team received during the previous night. He sees this as part of his job of preparing and strengthening the human engine, which he is using to complete the work. To keep the team fit and to work them hard is his job—and the beauty of it is that the more thoroughly he does it, the happier and more contented they are. These instincts of fierceness and winning out no matter what the obstacle are readily reactive to demand and most helpful to the manager who knows how to use them.

In some industries, the personal touch of the line manager (foreman) in direct contact with the team is necessary. He understands all the facilities offered, their advantages, and what management intends to do for the team, and he is there in close touch to see that they get the right ideas and make the most of them. He is the immediate manager who directs the thousand little things of the daily work, making his team feel his interest in their wellbeing, success, and job satisfaction.

Creating and Maintaining Order

The newly appointed manager is likely to have more nervousness about his ability to maintain order than about anything else in connection with taking charge of a team. He wonders if they will follow him and is not sure of himself as a leader. It will help to understand how order is maintained. It is often said that order is the result of the manager's administration of rewards and redirects. However, order is the result of the manager's entire demeanor and how he performs his job, of his personality and methods, of everything he does for his team, to his team, and with them.

Among all these, rewards and redirects play an important part. Rewards have a lot to do with building up order so that redirects are given much more easily and pleasantly. If the manager has established ethical leadership, he will rarely need to use any redirects. This has been proven repeatedly and with various occupational teams. In every phase of human endeavor, fair treatment and the encouragement that comes from the recognition of quality work will soon establish a culture that makes redirects out of place and unnecessary.

An example of the highest type of unyielding order based on purely self-governing principles is that of a highly trained college football team. Here we have individual skill and initiative highly developed, together with a sense of servitude, teamwork, and the requirements of leadership and discipline. Here we find instant, unquestioning, and cheerful respect to directions, which enables the team to tackle the toughest opponents. If you are a manager who needs an order of quick, unspoken compliance to instructions, consider the example of the football team as your model. Forsake coercive submission, which is unethical leadership.

Be Timely in Recognition

Probably the most effective reward is the subtle word of recognition of individual effort or excellence; sometimes even a nod and smile are enough. The main thing is to show the individual and other team members that you see and appreciate what he is doing. So, as you manage the work of your team, be on the lookout for chances to recognize individuals. Do not overdo it; flattering or unmerited praise does more harm than good. Keep it as a reward for excellence and make sure team members trust they will get it when deserved.

Do not be the manager who goes around assessing his staff, looking only for faults and speaking only to criticize something wrong. Be the manager who seeks quality work to laud it. Correct mistakes with the spirit of showing how it could be done better. If you are the first manager, you will hold your team to a certain level of accomplishment by a tremendous effort; if you become the second manager, you will soon have your team moving in the same positive direction. Davis cannot figure out why he cannot do as well as Miller, whom he heard the managers complimenting. Appreciation of an individual's excellence never fails to inspire continued effort to win further praise.

Influence of Reputable and Insufficient Staff

On every staff, you will find certain personnel of stronger and happier characters than the average people. These team members make the best of things and ease the rest along through the hard tasks; their influence is truly a great asset. The manager must note these staffers and do what she can to increase their influence with the others. If she must show favor to an individual, she should pick one of these staff members to receive it, allowing everyone to see her appreciation of their smiling, enthusiastic team spirit.

On the other hand, other staffers rumble and grumble, and their influence lowers the morale of the group. You must know these individuals also and do what you can to convert them to cheeriness and a will to win. Where an individual's influence is negative, be sure you do nothing to strengthen his standing within the group. If someone must complete an unpleasant task, it is often well to let that individual handle it. A manager who did not think of this and made the mistake of handing the reward to the negative individual would ruin the morale of the entire group by making them feel that integrity was not recognized and that their manager lacked good judgment.

Therefore, you must know your staff and monitor their work and their team spirit so that you may reward the deserving and never appear to support the undeserving. In a time of difficulty or stress, when the morale of your group is being tested, it will succeed or break down depending largely on which type of individuals have the strongest influence. It will be advantageous if you have strengthened the strong, cheerful ones and made them assistant managers with respect in your group.

Manager, a Teambuilder

The best thing about being a manager is the chance to build up the character of the staff—to embrace a team member, to discover his difficulties and areas needing improvement and also his strong points and potentials. This will not only bring you enormous satisfaction and personal reward, but it will also bring value to the organization and your team in that you have made this team member be all that he can. Several managers have found reward in taking a deep interest in the personalities of their supervisors and in making it their business to mentor and assist in building the business character of an individual who may have appeared an almost hopeless case in business.

Every manager is regularly affecting the future of his team, consciously or unconsciously. His influence on reward and redirect makes this inevitably true. His decisions and acts of authority each tend to strengthen or discourage the character of the person affected. This is what makes us tremble to see the power of managership in the hands of uninformed, dishonest, cruel, or even uncaring managers.

A successful manager realizes that by strict fairness, encouragement, and guidance, he may develop a quality team. And, likewise, by continued bias, he may break the team's spirit, destroy its confidence, and leave it a worse part of the organization than he found it. He accepts this responsibility and takes pleasure in trying to use his influence for the good of the team, department, and the organization. He is the ultimate teambuilder, and with that thought in the back of his mind, he studies his problem in a desire to act as a transformational leader.

The Manager's Responsibility

If, in the end, you decide that reprimand must be given, do it yourself. Do not let anyone interfere with the authority over your team or exercise it for you, if possible. You want them to look to you for impartiality and see in you the seat of authority under which they act and are responsible. This means that you handle every situation and make it clear that the decision as to the talking-to is the result of your judgment.

If the offense must be handled more severely than you are permitted to administer, only then should you send it to a higher authority—and with your recommendation. It is a lazy manager who allows others to reprimand or redirect his team. Only allow this if you are dealing with an unruly person who will not respond to fair treatment and is, therefore, a candidate for release.

Prompt Action Necessary

Since both rewards and reprimands have a major effect on an individual and on the team, action in both cases should be taken immediately following the instance while it is fresh in the minds of all. Ensure your team realizes that you take the job of managing seriously and that the conduct of each member is a matter of real interest to you. To overlook wrongdoings and inattentions that appear deliberate causes them to multiply and discourages the faithful members of the team.

The word or nod of recognition of acceptable performance is immediate and has its effect, so also does the immediate recognition or correction of wrongdoing. This first step may be a warning or even a redirect. Begin by calling the person to the office and ask his reason—and ask in a tone that assumes he has a reason and you intend to give it fair consideration. You may have to defer action until further investigation, but you have taken the first step and established the immediate effect. You should only continue to a decision if the circumstances dictate.

Symptoms of Poor Managership

Most of us have seen people in positions of authority who are awful examples of what a manager should be. A little authority in their hands seems to upset the balance in their heads. They lose all sense of how to deal with people, become ridiculously ignorant and loudmouthed, and unethical. They try to rule by fear, bullying, and physical force. They are the boss instead of the leader because they have been named the boss—yet they do not know how to lead. Their first step when they see anything going wrong is to yell, "What the heck are you doing?" in a tone that implies the person is not only a fool but a criminal. They disgrace every feeling of dignity he may have, assume his motives are those of a thief and a liar, and then expect him to respond with quality work and loyal service. Of course, that is ridiculous.

Such methods of control bring only hostile compliance and even invite open rebellion. Arrogance and rage are a thin disguise for incompetence, and it would be a good thing for these managers to realize the disrespect and disgust they are implanting in the hearts of their team. Some do not know any better and may need to be trained; others lack the strength of character and are hopeless. Neither should be left in authority as they are.

Misconduct: Fault of Manager

Where you find repeated cases of insubordination or indifference to respectable work, you will normally find that the cause for it lies in the presence of a manager who is not ethical enough for his job. This is true in most organizations. Remember, the average person desires to work hard and build a future for himself, so if several tend to go astray on a team, the answer is sure to be in something wrong with its manager. Likewise, where a manager finds himself unable to maintain order, he should look no further than within himself.

We often hear the statement, "I've got the worst bunch of supervisors in the business. No one could do anything with them." This is an admission of the manager's incompetence. Average human beings are subject to similar instincts and measured by the same basic principles. I have seen a team who were all but mutinous under a hard-headed, narrow-minded manger become one of the best-performing teams of the entire organization under a few weeks of new managership with one who embodied principles of fairness and decorum in treatment of people. The lesson is simple to the person who wants to be a successful manager and wants his team to achieve outstanding results.

The Object of Managership

To become a successful manager, one must understand that you have to build up and maintain a high level of fairness and impartiality, individual initiative, loyalty, and teamwork. Prioritize these traits to reach the highest level of effectiveness for the accomplishment of the task in view. Your team must keep these objects in mind as a guide in all that is spoken or accomplished. The achievement of these characteristics is a continual inspiration to a successful manager. By his comments and criticisms during the progress of the work and by his every act in administration, he seeks to build morale and initiative and all these essential qualities in his team.

In conclusion, as to the personal qualities required in the successful manager, we collectively ask that each manager intelligently use the ones he possesses. My list is not intended to compute all the best qualities of the great managers throughout history with the expectation that you adopt them as your own. We all have some sense of impartiality and fairness, are influenced by ethical leadership and mastered self-control, and can use our judgment and will power to achieve lasting results.

The point is to learn the value of our various qualities and to develop them by intelligent use. We are all human; let us admit it and act accordingly. And that would be an excellent first step toward success in managership because nothing is more inspiring than for your team to say, "Our manager is a real human being."

Thousands of mediocre managers have scarcely made it through one big job after another simply because they had little ability for inspiring the loyalty, initiative, and the good actions of their team. Many others of stronger business character, who have attained The Ten Habits of Highly Successful Managers, have done so with ease because they inspire, and even recognize, their team's efforts. It is not difficult to learn how to be a successful manager by acquiring the art of those who know how to inspire the enthusiastic efforts of others.

We are not discussing the high qualities of Superman or striving to attain the leadership of Abraham Lincoln. Not all these points will apply to every case of leadership, as in some cases many of them might be unreasonable. So as you read something that may strike you as unreasonable in the situation you have in mind, give it fair consideration and weigh it as a means of adding to your knowledge of the true spirit of a successful manager. The broader your knowledge and the better defined your individual opinions, the better judgment you will be able to bring to your managerial problems. In the end, what you believe, think, and feel will make you successful—or not.

BIBLIOGRAPHY

Building Character, Course in Business Essentials, Volume 4, Business Training Corporation, New York City, 1916.

Governmentwide Inclusive Diversity Strategic Plan, United States Office of Personnel Management, Office of Diversion and Inclusion, Washington, DC, OPM.gov, July 2016.

The Armed Forces Officer, American Forces Information Service, Department of Defense, NAVMC 2563, 1988.

Lincoln C. Andrews. *Manpower.* New York: EP Dutton & Company, 1920.

Printed in the United States
By Bookmasters